Great Teaching Moments

Great Teaching Moments

Edited by
Kendall Ayres

With a Foreword by
George D. Durrant

Bookcraft
Salt Lake City, Utah

Library of Congress Catalog Card Number: 90–62186
ISBN 0–88494–759–9

First Printing, 1990

Printed in the United States of America

Contents

Contents

Foreword

Many people—including me—refer to the compiler of this book as "my friend, Kendall Ayres." It is because of our love for Kendall and our love for teaching and learning that each of us whose words are included in this book responded to his invitation and remembered again a sacred time when we were part of a message written in a human heart.

As I read these several soul-stirring accounts, I was impressed that life itself is the great teacher. But life's experiences are sometimes neutral and, of themselves, lead people neither up nor down. It is in the interpretation of each experience, through inspired introspection, or by the gentle light focused by a caring teacher, that we are led to significant insights and to more complete joy.

Our divine Teacher fashions the perfect curriculum for each of us. At times he teaches us lessons directly, as he does in many of the fascinating accounts in this book. At other times he sends a teacher to help us see the meaning of the message. Is it any wonder, then, that the Lord seems to love the teachers who point the way to happiness in this life and to eternal life in the world to come?

It is because we help him teach his children that he seems so near us when we teach. There probably is no other area of life where so much could be written about God's holy inspiration and help than in the delicate and profoundly important task of teaching. Time and again on the pages that follow you will see and feel the Spirit of the Lord. You will sense, as does each contributing author, that God is very near when one is learning through an introspective heart, or in the family circle, or in the classroom. With just the slightest or with the mightiest request he enters in and, as Kendall says, "drives the nails"—nails that will build within us, and help us build within others, the joyous kingdom of our God.

GEORGE DURRANT

Preface

The carpenter goes to his job site every morning to build. He does not go primarily to listen to his radio, to take a mid-morning break, or to visit with his fellow-workers, but to build. Further, I suggest that the essential task of a builder or carpenter is the driving of nails. Oh, I admit that he saws, measures, twists, and pounds, but these activities, it seems to me, are incidental to the actual constructing process — which culminates in the driving of nails to hold portions together and, ultimately, to create an entity.

We have been sent to the earth late in the final dispensation to build the kingdom of God. I believe that the ultimate task in this particular construction project is teaching. Granted, there are many additional, appropriate activities to supplement this, but, at its heart, kingdom-building is teaching.

I am reminded, in fact, of another carpenter who built the kingdom. He was first, and most essentially, a teacher — a driver of nails.

This book is about driving nails. It considers how they have been driven by a variety of aspiring carpenters and it reviews some of the beautiful parts of the kingdom that have been constructed. Since we can't all enjoy resident training with outstanding tutors, perhaps working through these pages will serve as an absentee apprenticeship for some and help them improve their technique by observing the craftsmanship of others.

For years I have noticed that the impact of teaching always seems heightened when the learning takes place through the medium of an experience or a story. Whatever the essential nature of this phenomenon happens to be (and I have tried to pin it down), its reality remains an inescapable fact, and I have come to yield to its potential. In light of this, I have turned to the personal experiences of others in an attempt to make a contribution to the increasing level of teaching effectiveness in the Church.

This book is a collection of episodes—some tiny, some extensive —in which great teaching has taken place. Sometimes it is the teaching by the author that is described. Sometimes it is the author who is being taught. Sometimes the author is a bystander and fortunate observer. Frequently, I have found, it is a combination of these. As the accumulation process has taken place, I have been instructed and motivated by each episode. Each can be examined and "dissected" to get to its essential parts, which parts may then be used by the reader to help with a particular teaching situation that he or she may be facing.

It is also my hope that some of the experiences herein will cause deeper or perhaps renewed determination to teach and motivate those close to the reader. I have found that my vision increased as I have read and compiled these accounts. I have been expanded in capability as a teacher and have been driven to new effort. It has also been my experience that each of the episodes is worthy of several examinations. Without exception, I have discovered deeper or additional insight as I have read and reread.

This is a story book—but it is a book of stories that teach. And while the stories teach a variety of truths, if we look closely we find that they also teach us how to teach—to drive the nails. I hope that within these pages there are for you, indeed, great teaching moments.

1

The Spirit Teaches Scripture

JEAN ASAY

Our daughter was just beginning her sophomore year in high school. With all the excitement surrounding the first school dance of the year and with many of her friends going with dates, she became painfully aware of how long it would be before her sixteenth birthday—May 25. Her awareness was heightened when she, too, was invited to go to the first dance. She replied, with commitment, that she was waiting until she turned sixteen to date. But, she admitted later, it did seem like a challenge to miss all of the dances and date activities for the year ahead of her.

Two months later she was invited to attend another school dance, which had a number of daytime activities associated with it. Many of her friends were going, the appeal became more than she had anticipated, and finally she asked if she could accept this one date. She assured us that she did not intend to make it a regular thing, but wondered if this one time couldn't be an exception. The more she talked about it, the more she wanted to go, until finally, after a week of hoping that her desire would pass, we realized we needed to help her make the right decision and feel good about it—instead of our just saying no.

Jean Asay, the mother of four children, played a key role in the piloting of the Outreach Program in the Salt Lake City area and for a number of years was a volunteer with LDS Social Services. She has served in several Young Women and Relief Society presidencies. A former missionary to the West Central States, Sister Asay is frequently called on to do workshops on scripture study and, for some years, has been employed by the Church Educational System, in both a teaching and a secretarial capacity.

After much prayer and thought and sensing her deep feelings, we pondered the situation together one evening. I felt a little uncertain as I heard myself finally saying to her, "If you will take one week to study your scriptures with this question in your heart, and pray about it in a way that you can hear Heavenly Father's answer—not just your own desire, but Heavenly Father's answer—we will abide by your decision." I was somewhat surprised that I had put us in that situation, but I had felt impressed to say it. She assured me that she would do her best.

Less than a week later she came to us saying that she had made her decision. She said she had received an answer—but it was not the one she wanted. She had done as we had asked, and one night while she was reading, a passage of scripture was transferred off the page and into her heart by the Spirit. She knew not only that it was true but also that it had personal relevance for her at this particular time:

> Verily I say, men should be anxiously engaged in a good cause, and do many things of their own free will, and bring to pass much righteousness;
>
> For the power is in them, wherein they are agents unto themselves. And inasmuch as men do good they shall in nowise lose their reward.
>
> But he that doeth not anything until he is commanded, and receiveth a commandment with doubtful heart, and keepeth it with slothfulness, the same is damned. (D&C 58:27–29.)

The course, which had seemed so vague to her before, was now clear. She had no doubt. She was content.

In a moment of her life when I had the courage to step back and let scripture and Spirit blend their power in instruction, our daughter learned more profoundly than she ever could have from my feeble reasoning.

2

2

Follow the Guide

DIANE DONE

During the summer of 1988 I went to school high on the slopes of Mount Kilimanjaro, in Africa. There were no classrooms and no one was identified as our teacher, but I received some of the profound instruction of my life there.

At 19,340 feet, Kilimanjaro is the highest peak in Africa and is considered a very difficult climb, not because of its technical nature but because of its steepness and the fact that while climbing you pass through five separate climatic regions.

The formal beginning of our climb was at a place called Marangu, where the four of us who would be climbing together met for the first time and received our preliminary instruction. We were given three pieces of advice and were told that unless we heeded them we had no chance of making it to the top of the mountain. The first two suggestions were to go slowly but steadily during the entire climb, enjoying every aspect of it as we progressed, to be prepared for the different demands of each day, protecting ourselves appropriately. But, we were told, the first two rules were absolutely point-

Diane Done graduated from the University of Utah and is currently pursuing a master's degree in Middle East Studies. She has recently been employed as a staff assistant to Senator Jake Garn of Utah and currently works for the Church Educational System as a seminary instructor. Sister Done served a mission to the Netherlands and Belgium, has back-packed Europe twice, and has visited Africa, Egypt, Israel, and Turkey. She is a popular motivational speaker, traveling on a national basis, weekly, at the appointment of groups such as Illinois Vocational Education Association and the Future Business Leaders of America of Atlanta, Georgia.

less if we ignored the third: Follow your guide—do exactly what he tells you to. He has been up the mountain three thousand times. Don't try to outthink him—just do what he says. I made up my mind that I was going to follow that bit of advice.

As we started up the mountain the next day, led by our guide Winifred and dressed in shorts and T-shirts, I couldn't help but reflect on how much comprehension of the Savior there was in the experience. He had a mountain to climb, and while he certainly sensed urgency, he moved slowly enough up its awesome slopes to remain aware and responsive to those whom, because he loved them so much, he had come to serve. He also was prepared to meet the demands of each new day, with its unique set of challenges. This preparation had taken place over extensive previous time, and now he was able to approach situations protected and confident. It occurred to me, as I labored up rock-strewn paths, that there were times when I entered my days of living not nearly so well prepared as I was now for this simple climb. I sometimes charged boldly forth without the protection of personal prayer or private scripture study. I was protected here from the elements of the mountain by heavy clothing and boots and gloves, but how often had I forged ahead in life without listening for the promptings of the Spirit to insulate me from life's elements?

The first day we climbed from 5,000 feet to 9,000 feet and spent the night at Mandara Hut. By this time the climate had changed from hot and humid in the morning to quite cold in the evening, and we were now in the clouds. The next morning we continued up the mountain, dressed now in long pants and sweat shirts, and climbed to 12,500 feet. We spent the night at Horombo Hut, where it was very cold. The following day we went to about 14,500 feet, where Kibo, our base camp, was located. We arrived at about two o'clock in the afternoon and rested until midnight when Winifred woke us and told us it was time to start the final ascent.

As I stepped outside it was absolutely lightless except for the light cast by Winifred's lantern. I made it a point to be the first climber in the line behind him, and I was so intent on "following my guide" that I literally put my foot where his had been on each step I took up that last leg of the climb. As I worked my way up that mountain, counting on the path established and the light shed by Winifred, my mind again turned to thoughts of the Savior and how crucial his path and his light were to me.

As we came to the halfway point the nervousness I had felt, as I stepped out of our hut into total darkness four hours earlier, jelled. By now I was not feeling well at all. Nausea was setting in, and I was getting numb. The wisdom of the decision to make the climb up this mountain was becoming highly questionable. We were now rubbing one another's arms and legs to keep the circulation going, and as we resumed climbing after our brief rest I did something I had made up my mind not to do. Winifred had told us not to look up at the mountain. I decided to take a look anyway, despite the words of our guide, almost as if to see if there weren't some better route to follow to get to the top. I have been struck since by the overwhelming irony of that thought and by its occasional parallel in my life, where the Savior is my guide. I have occasionally looked for better routes.

When I looked up and saw the immensity of the mountain, in what was now semidarkness, and comprehended how much of it was still left to be conquered, I sank to my knees in tears. I vomited. My ears had begun to bleed. I vomited again. I had not, in my wildest dreams, imagined that I still had so far to go.

At this point the parallel between my guide, Winifred, and the Savior became very poignant. As I was lying there on the trail, crying, Winifred came to me. He didn't tell me that it had been a nice try but that now it would be all right for me to go back down and try again some other day. He did not allow me to be content with almost. He told me that I was strong and that I could do it. He encouraged me. He built me. He cradled me in his arms and began to massage my arms and legs. He reminded me that he had been there before, that he knew the mountain well, and that he knew that I could make it. And then he said that he would assist me—*in continuing toward the summit*—until I was ready to go on under my own power. After about ten minutes he lifted me up and began walking me up the mountain until I could continue on my own.

In the classroom of that mountain slope I learned, much better than I had ever known it, how the Savior functions. He comes to us when the mountain looms larger than our imagined capabilities. He doesn't soothe us with contentment for mediocrity, nor mock us for intermediate stumblings. He builds and strengthens and reassures by reminding us of our capability—a capability that he knows so very well, because he has climbed our mountains himself and because he knows us so well. Having turned us again in the direction of the summit, and with the beginnings of renewed hope and some expectation, he lifts and assists and provides power until we are ready to move ahead, again, by our own strength. In the process he has allowed us to discover our capability for ourselves and has allowed that growth take place—not that he caused it, but that he made place for it. We are now strengthened for the next part of the climb, and eventually for the summit.

All this I learned while being tutored in the things that matter most, while working my way up the slopes of Kilimanjaro to its highest peak, Uhuru. Translated, Uhuru means freedom.

3

Broken Heart

MICHAEL WILCOX

As a boy I spent many summers working on my uncle's ranch in Nevada. The work was hard, but for a young boy it was more fun than tiring. On occasion we rode out into the desert and brought back wild horses, a few of which were singled out to be broken. These were roped, and after considerable trouble a thick leather halter with a strong rope attached to it was buckled over their heads. The rope was then tied securely to a deeply buried and very strong cedar post. The horses, used to going where they wanted to and doing what they pleased, fought that rope desperately.

In my memory I can still picture those horses pulling back with all their might against the rope. With feet planted firmly, they would lay back and shake their heads from side to side until they were exhausted. Even then, worn down as they were, they would sometimes still not approach the post enough to let the rope go limp.

I asked my uncle why he did this. I had always thought you broke a horse by putting a saddle on him and riding until he knew you couldn't be bucked off. This was my image of the cowboy. My uncle taught me that first the horse must learn to lead (or be led); that if he always fights the rope he will never be broken, so we teach him, first, to lead. I watched my uncle, little by little, day by day, work with the

Mike Wilcox is the father of five children and has served as bishop, stake mission president, and high councilor. He has taught seminary and institute for the Church Educational System in Arizona, Canada, Colorado, and Utah, and religion at Brigham Young University.

horses until they stopped fighting the rope. When they were gentle enough to follow my uncle while he led them with the rope lying loosely in his hand, they were broken. At that point he was so sure that a horse would follow the most gentle of leads that he would let me hold the halter rope and lead the horse around the corral. I can still feel the texture of the cotton braids as they lay loosely in my hand. Never once did one of those horses pull back.

I forgot those memories until one day I was reading the words of the Savior to the Nephites. He told them he wanted of them a sacrifice—the sacrifice of a broken heart and a contrite spirit. When I encountered the word *broken* I did not think of torn valentines, or grief, or sorrow, or even repentance. There returned to my mind the feel of the rope laying gently in my hand and, prior to that, the image of a wild-eyed horse, shaking his head violently and desperately from side to side, straining with all his strength against that unyielding rope.

What was the Savior asking of the Nephites on that occasion? I don't believe he was advocating sorrow or grief—such a sacrifice would be to no purpose. I believe he wants us "broken" in our hearts—unresisting—ready to be led by the gentlest of leads and promptings. I believe he would like us to stop straining back against a gospel that cannot yield, spiritually exhausting ourselves in the process.

4

Focus

GERALD N. LUND

One day in my second year of teaching seminary we had been through the morning classes, had lunch, and were ready to start the next period, when an announcement came over the public-address system. Four students had sluffed class during third period to take an early lunch. They had gone to a fast-food drive-in and, as they were leaving it, ran a red light. A fully loaded dump truck hit the car. The collision killed two of the students outright, and the other two were in critical condition in the hospital. The announcement came just as the fifth-period kids were walking over to seminary from the school.

As they came in it was obvious to me that they were in deep shock. The news had electrified the school. Some of my students had been sitting next to the four in classes earlier, just before they had sluffed. One of my students had even tried to talk them out of going, but their response had been to try to talk him into going with them.

We had the devotional, and I had gotten about three sentences into my lesson on Old Testament history when I realized that there was so much emotion that I just stopped. I

Jerry Lund is the father of seven children and has served in numerous teaching positions in his ward, as high priests group leader, and as bishop. He has served as chairman of the Church Gospel Doctrine Writing Committee and of the Youth Correlation Review Committee. He has taught seminary and institute and has been the director of College Curriculum and the director of Teaching Support Services. Currently he is employed by the Church Educational System as a Zone Administrator. He is the author of six books.

decided just to let the students talk and express some of the things that were so deep in their minds and hearts. And then, interestingly enough, they began asking questions. "Where are they going to go?" "What are they going to be doing?" I simply said, "You know, those are interesting questions. But let me ask you something else. Where do you think they are right this moment? Do you think they have any feelings now, differently, about sluffing school?"

From there we went to Alma and the *Discourses of Brigham Young*, and read some things together about the spirit world. We saw that, although their bodies had been smashed and their lives taken, that which was *really* them was still alive somewhere. Those friends, who had been so close just hours before, still had feelings and emotions, and perhaps regrets.

The classroom then opened up into a forum of discussion about death, about the spirit world and what that was like and how it related to the choices we make. It turned into one of the most significant teaching experiences I've ever had, because our focus went right to the core of things that were immediately and intensely at the very center of their attention.

I saw one of the students from that class a year or so ago. We started talking, and she brought that day back to my memory. She said that she had never forgotten it and added, "Every time I read about an unexpected death, I think, 'Am I ready? Am I going to go into the next life without regrets? Or am I going to wish that I had not done what I was doing at the time?' " She, too, had been taught, ever so indelibly, by confronting an outgrowth of reality while in a setting of eternal truth.

5

. . . Until They Know We Care

ROBERT L. MILLET

My first experience with teaching seminary began with five classes of ninth graders. I entered the classroom with great expectations, to say the least. I had enjoyed teaching the gospel to nonmembers while on a mission, had taught the gospel doctrine class in Sunday School for a number of years, and felt that to be involved in a weekday religious education program would be the highlight of my life. In my loftiest moments I had anticipated walking into the room, inviting the Spirit of the Lord to be with us through prayer, and "holding hands with God" for an hour while I witnessed the Holy Spirit working wondrous changes in the lives of a group of eager and theologically thirsty young people.

Somehow reality took a different turn. I found a surprising number in each class to be disrespectful, rude, insensitive, and almost totally uninterested in the marvelous things I had prepared to share with them. They chattered and laughed and occupied themselves irreverently with other things all through the class. This went on day after day.

Bob Millet is the father of six children and was employed by LDS Social Services before turning to the Church Educational System. He has been a seminary teacher, an institute instructor, and a teaching support consultant. Employed by Brigham Young University as an associate professor, he is currently the chairman of the Department of Ancient Scripture. He is the author and/or editor of numerous books and articles on LDS history and doctrine. Brother Millet has been a bishop, a high councilor, and a stake president's counselor, and has served as a temple worker. In addition he has served on the General Church Curriculum Committee and on the Church Materials Evaluation Committee.

One afternoon during fifth period one of my more challenging young men came into class late; the lesson had started some ten or fifteen minutes earlier. He walked up to me with his hands behind his back, and, while grinning broadly, said, "Brother Millet, I brought you something."

I said, "OK, Bill, what is it?"

At that point he retrieved from behind his back a can of plastic foam. He covered me with the stuff—my face, my hair, my new suit of clothes. I can still recall the first thought I had at that moment: I don't remember Elder Packer's book, *Teach Ye Diligently,* dealing with a problem quite like this one.

I "quit my job" every afternoon for three months. My wife, Shauna, would buoy me up with, "Come on, now, you can do it. You have something to offer. Be patient with them."

My principal was understanding and sensitive to my soul-struggling. He listened each day at lunch and empathized with my dilemma. He was also quite a humorist. I remember his saying to me, "Bob, do you know what my behavioral objective was for today? It was to leave the classroom at the end of the day of my own free will and while standing on my own two feet." Although his understanding and ready laughs did much to assure me that others were likewise struggling, the pain known only to those who have a vital message but few listening ears pierced my heart regularly.

My prayers during those early fall months were pointed and direct. There was no beating around the bush here: "O God, please change these wayward youth. Please help them to appreciate me and my message. Please open their eyes that they may see." Such prayers were neither vain nor shallow; I was pleading from the depths of my soul. I meant what I said. My desires were not unrighteous; I wanted my students to come to love the scriptures and love the Lord as I did. Well, God is merciful and he does answer prayers. And so it was that eyes were opened.

It was during one of my prayers at night—a prayer in behalf of my classes—that the stirrings of change began: stirrings within my own heart. On that glorious day I learned a lesson that would serve me for life. Having expressed what I had planned to say, I allowed some additional time on my knees for pondering and reflection. After a few moments there came a desire for further prayer. My words reached beyond my thoughts and I began to learn much from what was said; prayer became more than petitionary—it became instructive. My thoughts turned to the young people I taught; my own feelings were swallowed up in a love for them which I had never known. I felt a great need to repent of self-centeredness and an overwhelming desire to express my love for my students. My prayers changed. My petitions were now such things as, "O Lord, help me to be worthy of these great souls, for I know that they are precious in thy sight."

I didn't sleep much for the rest of the night. Morning finally came, and as I knelt in prayer beside my bed in the early hours of the day I pleaded one more time with the Lord —but this time I asked that the feelings of the night before might be manifest in my teaching that day. As I looked over the class in first period my heart and soul went out to them in love, as though there had been an opening of the windows of heaven. I told them how much I loved them. I told them what a privilege it was to teach them. I asked their forgiveness for my impatience and my spiritual shortsightedness. As I looked into their eyes I saw similar feelings in them and knew that we had communicated. More especially, we had been edified and were rejoicing together. Discipline problems were few thereafter. Relationships blossomed during the rest of the year and lasting friendships were forged which I hope to renew again and again in this life and into the next.

Some years later I was studying the Book of Mormon when I discovered an incident which took on new meaning for me. After Alma and his missionary companions had discovered the doctrinally deplorable condition of the Zoramites, and just prior to their ministry among these apostates, Alma prayed in disgust, "O, how long, O Lord, wilt thou suffer that thy servants shall dwell here below in the flesh, to behold such gross wickedness among the children of men? . . . O Lord God, how long wilt thou suffer that such wickedness and infidelity shall be among this people? O Lord, wilt thou give me strength, that I may bear with mine infirmities. . . . O Lord, my heart is exceedingly sorrowful; . . . wilt thou comfort my soul, and give unto me success, and also my fellow laborers who are with me." Alma's prayer continued. Perhaps the Spirit of the Lord began to mold and shape and focus Alma's prayer further; his heart began to turn toward the Zoramites, not in revulsion but in reverence; not with bitterness but with benevolence. And thus Alma finally prayed, "O Lord, wilt thou grant unto us that we may have success in bringing them again unto thee in Christ. Behold, O Lord, their souls are precious." (Alma 31:26–35.)

Surely the message of the gospel—the message of peace and love—is communicated more effectively and incorporated more lastingly when the teacher is a vessel of love, when he or she has come to view from God's perspective those to whom the message is to be delivered. How truly appropriate is the aphorism, "People don't care how much we know until they know how much we care."

6

Teach Students—Not Lessons

SAM D. MORRISON

Several years ago I was called to teach a Sunday School class of twelve-year-olds. Since it was a new experience I went into it with vigor and commitment, and I felt that I was well prepared to give my lessons. My approach and attitude were that I was called as a teacher and that I was there to teach. I had topics that I wanted to cover and a lesson plan that I needed to follow. Yet as the weeks passed I found that I wasn't succeeding. It was a class of around twelve or thirteen students who were generally inattentive and unwilling to listen to the lessons. I found that I would be lucky to cover one-third of the material, since I had to frequently stop and ask for their attention and make comments about their rudeness.

My goal in teaching was to make sure I covered the whole topic each week and to show the knowledge I had. I wanted to teach directly and simply as, for instance, one would in teaching the proper crossing of the street: "First you must *stop*. Then you have to *look*. Finally you must *listen*."

I found that this approach just was not working, and after a year of teaching the class I felt I had failed. I shared my frustrations with some of the parents of those children. They didn't seem interested enough to be willing to do anything to

Sam Morrison is the father of four children and is currently serving as a bishop of one of the student wards at the University of Utah. He has been a stake executive secretary, executive secretary to the president of the Utah Salt Lake City South Mission, and a bishop's counselor. Brother Morrison is currently employed as the director of the Placement Center at the University of Utah.

make a difference in their children's behavior. I blamed class size. I blamed rowdy kids. I blamed myself. In retrospect, I have thought that it would have been better if I had been called as a friendshipper but not as a teacher.

A few years later I took a class offered by our stake in which the principle of inductive teaching was taught. In that class a master teacher taught us an approach that began by creating interest and understanding of general principles through the discussion of a familiar idea, and then by tying that understanding to a specific comprehension that was the real point of the presentation in the first place. However, this method struck me as being too indirect. It just didn't get down efficiently enough to the point that I wanted to reach. And yet, as years have passed, I have begun to realize that my matter-of-fact, rather clinical approach was forcing me and my agenda between the gospel truths and the students. What an irony! I was preventing *in the name of efficiency* the very connection I was called to make. I began to appreciate that perhaps one of the master touches that would have really helped that class of twelve-year-olds was this inductive teaching—and yet I would never have considered it because it wasn't direct and precise enough.

As I reflect back on that year I see many things I did wrong, but perhaps the most important thing was that I felt I was there to teach lessons, when in fact I was there to teach students and touch lives. I failed to recognize the role we have with students; instead my goal was to cover a lesson topic each week. Perhaps we all have such a vein within us. At least in my case I learned that the best way to teach is to be sufficiently interested in the people we're teaching to recognize that we are not there to present material but lessons. We are there to touch lives by offering to them gospel realizations.

7

Sight

KELLY HAWS

Not very long ago a young lady stayed after one of my seminary classes for a few moments. She said, "Brother Haws, can I talk to you?"

I said, "Sure."

We started to sit down together, but she said, "No, you'll need to get your scriptures." So I walked to the back of the room. While I was there she said, "Grab a red pencil, too, while you're back there." So I sharpened a red pencil and came back and sat down.

"Can I show you a couple of things that I've learned recently?" she began.

"Last night I was studying in the Doctrine and Covenants and came across a passage I was interested in. I don't remember now where that passage was, but I went to the footnotes and they referred me to the Old Testament, where I looked up a couple of things." And then, oddly enough, she said, "It was interesting, Brother Haws, because I read the Doctrine and Covenants passage I had been referred to, and I didn't understand it—and so I just kept reading. I came across some other things that I just have to share with you. Will you turn with me to Amos, chapter 4?" So we opened our Bibles to Amos, chapter 4.

Kelly Haws, the father of one son, graduated from Brigham Young University and earlier was studentbody president at Snow College in Ephraim, Utah. Kelly is an avid fly fisherman, a basketball enthusiast, and a keen reader of the Book of Mormon. He has been a bishop's counselor and is currently serving on a high council.

Then she said, "Now listen, Brother Haws, I don't want you to miss this." I turned with her and got out my red pencil and she said, "Okay, start in verse 6." So we started reading in verse 6: "And I also have given you cleanness of teeth in all your cities, and want of bread in all your places: . . ."

This is a young lady who has caught the vision of John 6 and the living bread that it teaches of, and of John 4 and the living water spoken of there, so whenever she reads *bread* she thinks *Christ* and whenever she reads *water* she thinks *living water* and his doctrines. The verse finishes: ". . . yet have ye not returned unto me, saith the Lord."

Then we began reading verse 7: "And also I have withholden the rain from you, when there were yet three months to the harvest: . . ."

Here she stopped me again. She wanted to make sure I didn't miss this, so she said, "Brother Haws, now listen really carefully; I don't want you to miss this. Listen, Brother Haws, I don't want you to miss it. '. . . And I caused it to rain upon one city, and caused it not to rain upon another city: one piece was rained upon, and the piece whereupon it rained not withered.' "

And she looked up at me with a big grin on her face, her eyes wide open, and hoping that I had gotten it, she said, "Did you get it? Did you get it? Did you get it, Brother Haws, did you get it? Did you see?"

I have to admit that I didn't really see it very well, so I said, "Please explain it to me. Tell me what you saw. Help me through it a little bit."

She said, "Don't you see, Brother Haws, the rain is living water, and where it rains, people live. In the passage, the piece whereupon it rained not—withered. Don't you see, Brother Haws, wherever living water is—where the Savior is —where his teachings and doctrines and words are, we live. And where it doesn't rain we wither." And then we finished, with verse 8: "So two or three cities wandered unto one city, to drink water; but they were not satisfied: . . ."

She said, "I think the two or three cities wandering to one city to drink water are like you and me going to each other as a source of living water. We know that we are not the source of living water, and so we are not satisfied." And then the Lord concludes: ". . . yet have ye not returned unto me, saith the Lord."

"Brother Haws, we know that he's the source of living water. When we go to each other we don't find living water —only when we go to Christ. Do you see it, now? Do you see it?"

I saw it.

At that point she shared with me something she had written in the margin of her Bible and I, in turn, wrote it in the margin of my Bible: "When men rely upon men they thirst, but when they return to Christ they are filled."

Then she said, "Brother Haws, can I share one more with you? Just one more. Do you have time?"

I said, "I sure do."

She said, "Okay, turn to Haggai."

I didn't even know people knew how to pronounce the word *Haggai,* let alone spend time reading the book, but she had, so I asked her where it was. She took me to it—to chapter 1, verses 5 through 7. It was almost a continuation of what we had been reading in Amos: "Now therefore thus saith the Lord of hosts; consider your ways. Ye have sown much, and bring in little; ye eat, but ye have not enough; ye drink, but ye are not filled with drink; ye clothe you, but there is none warm; and he that earneth wages earneth wages to put it into a bag with holes. Thus saith the Lord of hosts; Consider your ways."

She then said, "Brother Haws, when we sow much, if it's with each other or if it's in looking to man or the arm of flesh as the source, we bring in little. We can eat lots and lots of food, but if it's not the living bread we 'have not enough.' We can drink for ever and a day, but if it's not the living water that is offered from the fountain of living water, then we are not 'filled with drink.' We can clothe ourselves with everything but the right clothing, but we will stay cold. And we can seek to earn wages, but if they are not the wages of service to the Master they will ultimately be lost to us—just as surely as

19

coins in a bag full of holes. And then look, Brother Haws, how the Lord concludes just as he began, 'Thus saith the Lord of hosts; Consider your ways.'

"Do you see it, Brother Haws, do you see it?"

Oh yes, I saw it. I saw the profound truth she had taught me from the scriptures. But I also saw, by now, far more than even *she* realized. I recalled the words of a prophetic statement made by Commissioner of Church Education Henry B. Eyring to Church Educational System Administrators on April 6, 1981:

"I have a hunch, if you just want my prediction, that four or five years from now you will see more Latter-day Saint youth in our classes pondering the scriptures, talking about them with each other, teaching each other from them, loving them, believing that they really do have the answers to the questions of their hearts."

I saw, in addition to her insight, the greatness of her generation and the hand of the Lord moving through these times. What a sight!

8

Foundation

DAVID SODERBERG

One evening at dinner we called on our oldest child, Andy, to offer the blessing on the food and he began with the usual platitudes of a six-year-old boy. However, on this occasion he included a request which would, later in the evening, become profound. He asked Heavenly Father to bless us, that as he and I went riding on our Honda three-wheeler after supper we would be protected from harm. At the conclusion of the prayer, my wife and I looked at each other, pleased with what we viewed as a sincere request from this very young child, but thought little more of it.

At the conclusion of dinner, Andy and I went out riding in the hills south of our home on the family ATV. We stayed in the flat areas and in the very low hills because he was nervous about riding in the steeper hills. We had a wonderful time together, enjoying the riding and the companionship of father and son. As it grew dark we turned for home and decided to climb one more hill (which was a bit steeper than those we had been climbing), since it was a shortcut to home. However, we didn't have enough momentum to make it over the lip at the top of the hill, and when we got there the Honda just seemed to hover in mid-air. Then it began to roll backwards on top of us. Andy had been sitting in front of me, and as we fell backwards I just held on to him and diverted the

David Soderberg is the father of three children and has been employed by the Church Educational System for seven years. He has served in an elders quorum presidency, as a ward mission leader, and as a counselor to a stake mission president, and has held numerous teaching positions. He is a member of the South Jordan Planning and Zoning Committee.

weight of the Honda away from us with my feet so that it wouldn't land on top of us.

Although we weren't seriously hurt, Andy, who normally doesn't show much emotion, was almost out of control with fear, sobbing desperately. My mind was racing with thoughts of deaths and serious injuries that had resulted from accidents on ATVs and I, too, was extremely shaken. However, I was able to sit Andy on my lap and eventually calm him down. It was at this point that I made a comment, which I now believe was directed by the Spirit and which turned out to be the only thing that would get him back on the three-wheeler. However its impact went way beyond just getting him safely home that evening. I said, "Andy, tonight at dinner you asked for a special favor from Heavenly Father and neither one of us had any idea that we were going to need it. Do you believe that Heavenly Father protected us as you asked him to?"

He sat and thought for a second and I saw the realization come over his face. He knew that a prayer had been answered. I had been trying merely to get him back on the Honda so that we could get back to the house. Instead Andy experienced, for the first time in his life that he could identify, the tangible results of his Heavenly Father responding to an earthly request.

Well, he did get back on with me, and we rode home. But I know of the depth of impact of those moments, because since that time his verbal testimony has changed from, "I love my Mom and Dad and I believe the gospel is true," to "I know the gospel is true and I know that Heavenly Father answers prayers." That incident has served as a foundation not only for conviction but also for a continuing dialogue between the two of us on gospel subjects. How grateful I am for those moments of instruction, which have formed a basis for my son's growing testimony of the reality of the restored gospel.

9

The Moment Long Awaited

KENDALL AYRES

They had been coming to my office all day long. All were involved in the school play in one way or another, and all of them were either very frightened or deeply concerned. It seems that one member of the cast had been involved with satanism for some time and had taken the occasion of the play rehearsals to bring her Ouija board to school and to invite some fellow cast members to "experience" it with her. This had gone on for several post-rehearsal sessions, until those she had introduced to the powers of evil had experienced enough to know for themselves that these powers are very real. That morning, the day before opening night, the girl had come to school and had quickly let it be known that the Ouija board had communicated to her that there would be some sort of tragedy associated with the opening of the play and, further, that one particular girl named Pat would die.

At that time in her life, Pat, though one of our seminary students, was having her struggles in living the gospel. When she was informed of the threat she came into my office with one of her friends. She was in tears and nearly out of control with fear and wanted to use the phone to call her dad. I knew most of what had been going on by that time, but the threat directed at her had not come to my attention until then. She told me of the death threat and of her great, great fear of

Kendall Ayres is a convert to the Church and the father of seven children. He has been employed by the Church Educational System for twenty-two years as a seminary instructor and principal and is currently the teaching support consultant for the southern third of the Salt Lake Valley.

going home—or of doing anything, for that matter. This girl was petrified. She knew from the few experiences she had had the previous few days that there were some very real powers involved, and she wasn't prepared to deal with those powers. On top of all that, the safeguards that she had been taught all her life by faithful parents had been rendered useless by the life she was living, and she knew it. She was spiritually helpless.

She called her dad, who was a paramedic and on duty at the time, and tearfully pleaded with him to come and get her. This man, who understood rescuing those in peril, was a great priesthood bearer and a greater father. He loved this struggling daughter deeply. He did not hesitate. He knew that inconvenience and bad timing and all the other concerns of the world were suddenly of no consequence. He was in my office in very short order, still in his uniform—ready to help his frightened daughter.

And there she sat, anxious now for his protection and his wisdom. How long had he waited for that moment? How many times had he reasoned and pleaded and prayed? I couldn't possibly know, but what followed indicated without doubt that it was a long-awaited and anxiously anticipated opportunity.

He first got her to rehearse back to him all that had happened and all that concerned her. He then assured her that he, as a bearer of the priesthood—the very power of God—would not allow harm from evil sources to come to her. He then reminded her that she could have been safe even without his help if she had been living the kind of life that allowed that protection to be provided. But since they both knew that she wasn't living that life, he suggested that they stop by the bishop's house (who he "happened" to know was home) on the way to their own home, so that she could share with him anything that was out of line in her life and, therefore, begin to restore her ability to provide her own protection against the powers of the adversary. He was a very wise father.

I wondered again to myself—as I had been privileged to watch this magnificent priesthood bearer clothed in his worldly attire yet functioning on a celestial level—how long he must have waited for that moment of fertility.

10

To Thine Own Self Be True

STANLEY A. PETERSON

Late one night my son, who works at a drive-in movie theater, came home rather disturbed and bewildered. He informed me that he had backed his car around to pull out of the theater, didn't look behind him as well as he should have, and had run into a parked car. He was obviously upset about the damage he had done to both cars, and about the fact that he would have to bear the responsibility for the accident and the cost above that which our insurance would cover. But he was even more disturbed over what had taken place after the collision.

As he went to the other car, a lady got out and told him that she had gone to the movie to meet her boyfriend. Unfortunately, this woman had not only a boyfriend but also a husband, and she indicated that it was very important to her that her husband not know that she was at the theater. Therefore, she told my son, since he had run into her and caused this problem, she wanted him to go with her to a local grocery

Stanley Peterson is the father of six children and is currently the administrator of Religious Education and Elementary and Secondary Education for the Church Educational System. He has been the dean of Continuing Education at Brigham Young University, as well as the associate commissioner of Religious Education and Schools and the director of Continuing Education for the Church Educational System. Prior to his employment with CES, Brother Peterson was a teacher and principal in the public education system in southern California. He has served as a bishop three times and as a member of a stake presidency. He has also been a member of the Aaronic Priesthood MIA general board and of the Melchizedek Priesthood General Committee of the Church. He is currently serving as a member of the Church's Correlation Executive Committee. In 1971 he received recognition as one of the outstanding young men of America.

25

store parking lot and set up the accident so that it would appear to have taken place there. She then wanted to report the circumstances to the police under those conditions, without mentioning the drive-in theater, thus avoiding any difficulty with her husband.

My son would not agree to lie about what had happened and, at his refusal, she suggested that she would be the one to tell the story, so that he would not have to be the one who would lie to the police. However, he still would not agree to the setup and falsification of the circumstances and finally told her simply that they would have to report the incident to the police. Since it had taken place on private property, they determined that they would go to the police station to make the report.

Thus my son had come home to talk to me and to get my support before facing the confrontation at the police station. We talked about the circumstances and he told me that even though he knew his carelessness was going to be the cause of considerable difficulty for the woman, he was still not willing to be dishonest. He added that the pressure was increased by the fact that not only had she pleaded for his cooperation but also she had actually become very angry at him when he indicated that he would not be a part of her deception.

I told him I would go to the police station with him and we would face it and work things out together. When we arrived we found that she was already there and in the process of reporting the incident as though it had taken place in the grocery store parking lot. Now my son not only had to tell the truth, counter to the wishes of the woman, but also, in doing so, had to make clear the fact that she was filing a falsified report with the police.

As Mark realized what was developing, he gave me a rather bewildered look and said, "How do I handle this, Dad?"

I responded, merely in support of what I already knew to be in his heart, "You know what you have to do, son. You stand up for what you know is right and tell the truth as you have planned to."

When the woman had completed her version of the story, Mark, with some fear and trepidation, told his, which was, of course, completely counter to everything she had just said. The awkwardness of the situation was compounded by the fact that she was a good ten years his senior, thus increasing her theoretical credibility, and by the fact that the cause of all of the difficulty was his own personal carelessness. However, he stood undaunted, reported the incident exactly as it had actually occurred, admitted his fault in the matter, and indicated that he would bear the resultant financial responsibilities.

Once Mark had told his side of the story and exposed the falsification, the woman, angry but embarrassed, admitted that he was telling the truth. The police then gave her a very harsh reprimand about the consequences of filing a falsified report with the police. Her inaccurate account was both in written and oral form and so they made her begin all over again and do both a second time. She was not happy.

The situation was a very difficult one for my son to work his way through, but I was more proud of him than words can express for the way he handled it. Not once during all the pressure and awkwardness did he question what he had to do. That was never the issue. He knew what was right and never wavered in it. The only question in his mind was how to proceed and handle the details. For that, and that only, he had come to me for help. I was only too happy to assist.

I learned, that night, not only that he had been listening as his mother and I had tried for all those years to teach to him the eternal truths that would bring him the greatest happiness, but also that he had made them his own. He no longer needed us to help him establish his rights and wrongs. I also learned that we had been blessed to have, as our own for the eternities, one of the great souls that our Heavenly Father has sent. What an awareness became mine that night as I was taught so profoundly by a young man who had no idea that he was instructing his grateful father, but was merely trying to remain true to himself!

11

Perspective

TED SANDSTROM

A short time ago our five-year-old boy lost the companionship of his grandfather whom he adored and with whom he had spent countless hours. They had enjoyed together all the aspects of life that a grandfather has to offer a little boy. The death came suddenly and took all of us by surprise and, of course, afforded no opportunity for preparation. During the process of taking care of arrangements and trying to respond to the deluge of varied feelings, I found an occasion to take him aside and to ask if he knew what had happened and where his grandfather was.

When the little boy asked, in response, if his grandpa was still lying out in the field, I was provided an opportunity to teach a lesson about death and resurrection and the relationship of body and spirit. I used the visual example of a hand in a glove, and explained that the body and spirit were united when they were born and now they were separated. I explained that the glove represented that which we would put into the ground and that the spirit was in a place where it awaited the opportunity to put the glove back on, as it were. He seemed to be satisfied with that explanation. He was, perhaps, more comfortable than most of the adults who were around him, in being able to understand. I attribute that to

Ted Sandstrom is the father of four children and is the fire chief of South Jordan, Utah. He has served as a bishop, high councilor, and Sunday School president and has held many teaching positions. He is currently employed as the assistant principal of the Alta Seminary in Sandy, Utah, having been with the Church Educational System for nineteen years.

the fact that little ones seem to be so close to the Spirit and so teachable.

A few days after the services and the burial had taken place our little boy was with us in family prayer and it was his turn to offer the prayer. He said the usual things about blessing Mommy and Daddy and keeping everyone safe, and then he said, "Please tell Grandpa that I love him and that I miss him and that I can't wait to see him again." And then, almost in a postscript, he added, "And Heavenly Father, we'll take care of the glove if you'll take care of Grandpa."

What an opportunity it was for me to gain perspective from one who was so much closer to the source than I! I suspect that we are continually experiencing marvelous moments from which there is much to learn. I would hope that we would more frequently take advantage of those experiences and recognize God's hand in all that we have and in all that is available to strengthen us.

12

First Seek to Obtain My Word . . .

NAME WITHHELD

Recently I was asked by my son to take him to a Scout meeting. I was almost reluctant to do so because I had other matters pressing, but, I am now thankful I agreed to do so. As I dropped him off he asked if I would return around nine o'clock to pick him up. At the appointed hour I was back, and when he got into the car he looked at me and asked if I had been waiting long. I replied that I hadn't.

As we pulled away from the curb he asked whether, instead of going straight home, we could drive around for a few minutes. I answered that that would be fine. When I asked him why, he said that he had some concerns that he had been wanting to talk about, but that he hadn't been quite ready to do so until now. He then began to confess some things that he had done. This young man, who had some understanding of repentance, purged his soul that night beside me in the car as I drove. I listened most intently. As we pulled up in front of the house the process was not completed, so we sat in the car and he continued to talk until he had shared all that was in his heart.

Having finally gotten into the open the burden that had been tearing at him for some time, this wonderful boy turned to me, looked into my eyes and said, "Dad, after what I have done, what do you think the Savior thinks of me now?"

What a moment that was! This great young man, who understood the process of repentance but did not yet know its author, was poised for understanding. The burden was now mine and I earnestly sought the appropriate response. In my anxiety to identify an answer for him, I reflected on all that I knew of the Savior through my own experience. Scriptural discoveries passed through my mind as did personal experiences and the comprehension of the Savior I had gained as our relationship had developed through the years. I felt that I knew him, personally, well enough to represent him to my son; and, therefore quietly, but with deep conviction, I responded, "I want you to know, regardless of what you have done, the Lord loves you very, very much and he feels that same way even now."

I put my arms around him and he put his around me and, as we both sobbed, he said, "Dear Dad, how much I love you!" What a sense of overwhelming gratitude I had then, and feel even now, that I knew my Savior well enough myself to characterize him to my son. I have asked myself what I would have said or what I would have done if I had not had that relationship and understanding. I do not know the answer.

13

Innocence

TERRY OLSON

When I was growing up the youngest member of our family was my brother Philip, who had Down's syndrome. Although he certainly had limitations, he took the gospel very seriously, continually asking questions about things such as Joseph Smith and repentance. Even at that, we had reconciled ourselves to the fact that he didn't have a responsible enough mind for formally becoming a member of the Church. However, the thrill of his life came the day the bishop, who had consulted with the First Presidency, asked him if he would like to be baptized. Perhaps the only emotion equal to this came a few years later, when the bishop again called him in and asked him if he was ready to be ordained a deacon. He could hardly believe it.

Some time later he was called in by the bishop and asked if he would like to be ordained a teacher. Instead of responding with the cheerful excitement that was expected, Philip frowned and lowered his head in deep thought. When the Bishop asked him what was wrong, Philip responded, "I guess that would be okay—to be ordained a teacher—but would it be all right if I still passed the sacrament?"

Terry Olson is the father of six children and is the chairman of the Department of Family Science at Brigham Young University. He is the former associate dean of the College of Family, Home, and Social Science at that university. He has served, under Ronald Reagan, on a presidential commission to consider youth, morality, and pregnancy. He is a consultant with numerous school districts on the subject of implementing morality into public education and is the coeditor of two books on counseling written from an LDS perspective and the author of numerous family-related articles. Brother Olson is currently serving as a stake president.

The bishop said, "I think we can arrange that."

When Philip died in an accident at the age of twenty-three, his folks determined that he would be buried in Albuquerque, New Mexico, even though the family had been living in Orem, Utah, for about a year. He had grown up and lived in Albuquerque for most of his life. The first Sunday following the burial and memorial service my mother returned to attend church in our old Albuquerque ward. She had always sat in the chapel where Philip could pass the sacrament to her—he always received the same assignment in his positioning with the other deacons. She sat in the same place that morning, sang the sacrament song, and listened as the prayer was said. Then, inadvertently and out of habit, she looked up in anticipation of Philip coming toward her with the tray, and noticed for the first time that the deacons had left his position empty.

Years later, in conversation with my mother, the bishop reflected that the only time every deacon in the deacons quorum had gone on to serve a mission was during the years that Philip had been in the quorum with them. He noted that during those years, every time he had had an interview with any of those boys and asked them about their testimony, they always mentioned that Philip had something to do with the development of that testimony. Somehow, their association with his innocent enthusiasm for his calling had taught them, in ways they perhaps did not comprehend at the time, the eternal significance of what they were about.

14

It Grieveth Me That I Should Lose This Tree

KELLY HAWS

One year we had a unique set of young men in school who were very close friends and who did almost everything together. Although they were but sophomores at the time, it was evident that they would become the heroes of the school by their senior year, since they were athletes and quite popular. They came from great families and were outstanding young men. As they entered their junior year of high school some division of the group began to take place. Some of them decided that the most important influence and aspect of their lives was their Heavenly Father, while the others, although still fine young men, began to focus their lives on athletics, to the exclusion of much else.

Toward the end of their junior year we started looking for students to serve on our seminary council for the following year. One of the members of this group of friends, named Mike, was asked to be the president and another, named Tyler, was asked to serve as his assistant in the presidency. Thus the division of the group was deepened. This was further emphasized the following fall, when the two council members met in their own seminary class, which was designed specifically for members of the council.

A third friend, named Ted, although he remained friends

Kelly Haws, the father of one son, graduated from Brigham Young University and earlier was studentbody president at Snow College in Ephraim, Utah. Kelly is an avid fly fisherman, a basketball enthusiast, and a keen reader of the Book of Mormon. He has been a bishop's counselor and is currently serving on a high council.

with Mike and Tyler, was one who allowed athletics to become his primary focus. He went through quite a period of fluctuating between spiritual highs and lows. As the process of riding the spiritual roller coaster continued, he found the Church becoming less and less important in his life. At the same time he was pursuing a scholarship, so athletics became more and more important to him.

One of the things we have sought to establish in our classes is an atmosphere and a skill pointed at encouraging the reception of personal revelation in conjunction with the scriptures. As this process proceeds the students have a great desire to share their experiences with each other. They are offered an opportunity to do so at the beginning of most class periods, with the invitation, "Did anyone find anything in their personal study yesterday that they would like to share with us?" The response is that for ten to fifteen minutes the students teach each other from the revelations of the scriptures that they have received personally. This experience is particularly rich in the class that is made up solely of members of the seminary council.

As Ted's senior year progressed, we became concerned that we were losing him. He began putting God second in his life—then third, then fourth . . . His attendance at seminary became sporadic, as did his personal study of the scriptures.

At about the time this concern for Ted became quite pointed we found our attention drawn to the fifth chapter of Jacob in the Book of Mormon by one of the members of our faculty, who had had a significant experience with this passage during his family home evening. He had assigned each member of his family to go to his own room to read Jacob 5 and look for his own impressions and feelings.

When the family members came back together his eleven-year-old son said that he noticed that the Lord repeated the phrase, "it grieveth me that I should lose this tree," several times in the chapter. He commented that if he had lots of trees he couldn't feel too bad if he lost just one, because he had so many others. Then he insightfully observed that he didn't think the Lord was talking about trees. He felt that the Lord was talking about people—his sons and his daughters—and that *that* is why he had felt bad about losing even one.

This experience prompted a discussion, among members of our faculty, about Jacob 5 as a pattern for recovering those who are weakening—the taking of a withering, dying branch and grafting it back into a living, breathing branch in an attempt to save the dying branch. As we considered this principle, we asked ourselves why we couldn't apply it to our concerns for Ted and "graft" him into the seminary council class. In our first period we would then have the thirteen or fourteen members of the seminary council—and Ted. We hoped that the power of the word, as found in his friends' testimonies and in the scriptures, would have an impact on Ted and restore this dying branch. We enrolled him in the class.

Three or four months later we held, as we always do at the end of the school year, a combined testimony meeting for all of the class periods, in which all of the students came together in a general assembly to share their testimonies with each other.

Toward the end of the meeting Ted walked to the front of the room and bore his testimony. He recalled the first day when he entered that seminary class of council members and heard the invitation to share personal revelations, received through scripture, with the rest of the group. He had been shocked to see ten or eleven hands shoot into the air in order to gain the opportunity to share their recent experiences with the Spirit with their peers. He saw his best friend, fellow athletes, dating buddies, the most popular girls—all anxious to share insights and principles that had been discovered in scripture. As they shared with each other, in this manner, he spent the next several minutes astonished, completely taken aback, at what these people, whom he knew so well, had that he didn't have. He reported that the next day the same thing happened and that after several days he decided that if his friends could have this kind of experience, he could too. He started to read the scriptures again.

He concluded his testimony by telling us that he had decided to go on a mission. He thanked his friends and then his Father in Heaven for the powerful witness of the truthfulness of the Book of Mormon—which had not been his three months earlier.

We all learned once again that J. Reuben Clark was right when he said, speaking of young people, "They sense, by the spirit they have, that the testimony they seek is engendered and nurtured by the testimony of others" ("The Chartered Course," p. 6).

15

Groves

BERT HOFFMAN

As I left home that warm sunny morning I had no idea it would be one of those days a parent longs for in which he gets a glimpse at what is going on inside one of his children. For years we had prayed and taught and borne testimony in an ongoing effort to pass on to our children the faith we had found ourselves as converts to the Church. On this day I would get a glimpse of the impact.

Bert was dutiful and upright, often called a good son. He was always a pride to his mother and me, as well as a growing strength to his ward and quorum. We had driven for the hour or so it took to get from our home in LaGrangeville to priesthood meeting in Bridgeport, in the adjoining state. After that stop we had traveled the additional hour it took for us to attend Sunday School in Westchester; and now we were on our third leg, going to Sacrament meeting in the small branch at West Point, before the ride back home. It had already been a long day for a high councilor and his son on a Sunday filled with Church business.

When we began our journey the car was filled with conversation—a dad and his son together, getting caught up on things. We had enjoyed the day to that point. We very much

Bert Hoffman is a convert to the Church and served a mission in Korea shortly after his conversion. He has been employed for twenty-six years by the Church Educational System as a seminary and institute instructor and administrator. During this time he has been the director of the institutes at West Point, Columbia, Princeton, and Yale. He has served as bishop and high councilor, has been a PTA president, and has served on a number of school district educational committees.

liked being together—just the two of us. And it had been good to meet with friends—his from the youth programs, as well as mine from Church service. And we both looked forward to being with the Cadets, as we always did.

But now the car was quiet. The two and a half hours of driving had used up all our conversation, and I was absorbed in the driving and in the beautiful part of the country we were going through—Westchester County.

I don't recall how long it had been quiet, and I hadn't noticed the depth of thought our son had been involved in, but then it came: that question, the startling question that would let me see into his soul, the question that would also send me to the depths of my soul for an answer.

"Dad," he said, turning his face toward mine and bringing me back to our world within the car. "What if . . . what if the Church isn't true?"

There it was—my magnificent glimpse into this son's soul. Part of the message was that all these years of effort were working. He really was giving serious thought to all the things we had been saying. He really was trying to know. The joy that filled me in that moment was exquisite. And then I realized he was asking a question: "What if the Church isn't true?" And he expected an answer from me.

In that instant all my years of teaching flashed through my mind. All the thousands of classes I had stood before were present. From the depths of my soul I cried, "O God, help me teach like I have never taught before. Help me teach this, which I know to be true, to my son, who is wrestling to know. Help me teach this—to *your* son." And I waited.

There were no bright lights or magic messages that appeared on the windshield. Just a calm feeling, which seemed to say, "Go ahead. You know what he needs to hear. You know what he needs to do. Just go ahead."

I had always tried to give our children's significant questions the dignity and attention they deserved, and that is what I felt I needed to do with this one, also. So I began.

"Well, if the Church isn't true we're wasting a great deal of time and effort, and I doubt that it would be worth what we would get out of it. It's too expensive for a country club.

"But you know what your mother and I know. It is what you have been hearing for years and years. And it's the same thing your teachers have been saying.

"Now you're faced with a problem Joseph Smith was faced with as a boy. He had heard a lot of ideas, from a lot of people—and what did he finally have to do?"

Thoughtfully Bert answered, "He had to pray."

"Yes, and do you see that your question is the same as his?"

He nodded affirmatively and I continued, "He had to find a place where he could be alone and ask God for himself. And that is what you need to do. You know, you're about the same age Joseph was when he wondered. Maybe it's time you found your own sacred grove."

He raised his eyebrows quizzically, nodded his head again, and went back to his thinking.

We continued on to West Point—and what a glorious day it was!

He has since been to his grove.

16

To Know Enough to Do

DENNIS TENNEY

During the early fall of 1970, in the city of Arequipa, Peru, my missionary companion and I began teaching the discussions to a well-to-do businessman who had a tremendous thirst for truth. Because finding someone with substantial spiritual and financial capabilities as well as leadership potential was a rather rare opportunity, we felt extremely fortunate.

Night after night we taught this good man discussions that often lasted into the early hours of the morning. His appetite for truth was insatiable. In an attempt to help him we gave him *Jesus the Christ, A Marvelous Work and a Wonder*, and many pamphlets and other Church literature—which he absolutely devoured. His reading was always followed by endless questioning.

Nevertheless he remained noncommittal when we challenged him to be baptized. He thanked us profusely for helping to answer his questions, yet felt no strong need to commit himself to baptism. At the same time his family and friends derided him and questioned his interest in such a strange sect as Mormonism. It seemed that, because of his potential, the devil was determined to keep him out of the Church at all costs—even if it meant convincing him that he could live

Dennis Tenney is the father of four children and has been a financial consultant for many years. He has traveled internationally for a number of multi-national firms and, consistently politically active, is currently a member of the city council of Sandy, Utah. Brother Tenney has served in both a stake Young Men presidency and a stake mission presidency as well as having been a ward mission leader and an assistant high priests group leader.

comfortably in both worlds without the necessity of the commitment to baptism and active membership. My companion and I fasted innumerable times on behalf of this brother. It seemed that we were in a spiritual tug of war against the forces of evil and that the side with the most endurance was eventually going to win. However, we knew that if he did not commit himself to baptism we simply were going to have to spend our time elsewhere and move on to teaching others during the time we had set aside for him. We had long since completed teaching the standard discussions to him.

In what we had decided was going to be the last discussion we could allow ourselves to have with him, we opened with prayer and felt prompted to ask him how his reading of the Book of Mormon was progressing. He responded that he really hadn't gotten into it. We stopped the discussion and challenged him to read at least fifty pages before reading anything else and to pray fervently about it. We closed with prayer and left promptly.

Several days later, at the appointed time, we came timidly to his home, somewhat fearful that we had perhaps been too brusque and impolite at our previous appointment. After exchanging pleasantries and then opening with prayer, we asked him how he was progressing with his reading of the Book of Mormon. He lit up with an enthusiasm I had never before seen and tore the book open to a particular passage. After reading it out loud he turned quickly to some other passages and read them excitedly. He repeated this process over and over and finally exclaimed solemnly, "No man could have written this book without being divinely inspired! It is simply impossible otherwise!" That evening he committed himself to baptism. Only through his reading of the Book of Mormon did he gain the conviction to enter the Lord's kingdom and to do the will of the Father and *take action* to keep the commandments.

We walked away that night humbled and reminded that nothing can replace going directly to the Book of Mormon, with its attendant promise and witness, when we are seeking the pure knowledge that changes lives. In a single moment our investigator saw the light and we were profoundly reminded of its source.

17

Starting Where They Are

GEORGE DURRANT

Several years ago I was teaching seminary to Indian students at the Intermountain Indian School in Brigham City, Utah. These wonderful young people couldn't come to seminary during the day, so they all came over to the seminary building at once, right after school. I was one of several teachers who taught a portion of the total number. Mine was a class of about twenty twelve- and thirteen-year-old boys, and they were a real challenge, even on the best of days.

One afternoon I was walking to my classroom in order to be ready for them when they arrived. The phone rang at that moment. I answered it and found that it was one of the other teachers. She asked me, because she had an emergency and needed to stay home, to take her class of ten more young men. Again I headed toward the battle (or should I say the class). I found the other teacher's ten students and directed them to my classroom door. Just then I realized I had forgotten my supply box. I went back to my office to get it. By the time I got into the classroom there were Indian boys under the chairs, behind the curtains, and in the closet. They were

George Durrant is the father of eight children and the author of numerous books. A highly sought-after public speaker, he has served as branch president, bishop, Regional Representative, mission president, and president of the Missionary Training Center in Provo, Utah. Brother Durrant has assisted in writing family home evening manuals and served as a member of the Melchizedek Priesthood Committee of the Church and as director of the Priesthood Genealogical Department. He has been employed by the Church Educational System in the seminaries and institutes and has taught at Brigham Young University.

in no frame of mind to be taught what I had prepared for them—which was a lesson on the plan of salvation.

I went to the front of the classroom and offered a silent prayer that I might find a way to teach these, my dear young friends, whom I loved with all my heart. I tried to call them to order, but only a few heard and fewer responded. I then noticed that two of the boys in the front row were reading a comic book. I sat down by them and looked at the book. It was about cowboys. The frames they were reading showed two villains trying to shoot a third cowboy, who must have been the good guy. The two villains were on either side of the good guy, and as they shot, the good guy ducked and each villain's bullet flew over the good guy's head and hit the opposite villain.

I asked the two boys if I might borrow the comic book for a minute. They agreed. Then holding the open book high above my head I shouted to the class, "I am so sad!" After pausing I added, "I need your help with a problem I have run across in this comic book. Will you please help me with this? I don't know what to do about this problem and I really need your help. Who would be willing to help me?"

The thirty boys, seeing the comic book high above my head, became curious. They came out from behind curtains and out from under chairs and into their seats as I continued saying, "Please help me!" They came to full attention.

I then said, after reading from the comic book and showing them the story in its entirety, "I don't know what's going to happen to these two men who have just been shot and are now dead—and I'm sad for them and I'm worried about them. What's going to happen to them?" No answer. "What does happen to people when they die? Are these cowboys dead forever? Will they go to heaven?"

From that point a lively discussion ensued concerning life after death and the plan of salvation, and I was able to teach them the precious message. It was one of my great teaching moments.

18

Conduit

JEFF SWANSON

In February of 1989 I received a call at West Seminary in Salt Lake City asking that we host two men from the eastern United States who were associated with a national organization whose focus was to promote the separation of church and state. Their visit was prompted by a problem that a seminary had had in the southern part of the Salt Lake Valley. Some students, during a missionary week, had become overly zealous and had gone into the adjacent public school to talk to friends about the gospel. These men were concerned, therefore, about the role that seminary plays in the public school system in Salt Lake City, and, appropriate to their charge, felt the need to observe firsthand. Thus, they had been invited out by the Church to see for themselves.

An interesting agenda had been planned by the Church for these gentlemen during their visit. They had the opportunity to meet with several non–Latter-day Saint school administrators; several ministers in the area; the head of curriculum for the Church; Church Commissioner of Education J. Elliott Cameron; former Utah governor Scott Matheson; James Moss, the State Superintendent of Schools; and Palmer DePaulis, the

Jeff Swanson is the father of five children and has been employed by the Church Educational System for eighteen years. He has been a seminary principal in Las Vegas, Nevada; in Mesa, Arizona; and in Salt Lake City, Utah. A convert to the Church, he has served in a bishopric, on a high council, as an elders quorum president, and as a stake missionary, as well in many teaching capacities. As a young man he was deeply involved in politics. He has been published in the Utah Historical Quarterly, *being awarded recognition for the best article of the year on one occasion.*

mayor of Salt Lake City. In the midst of their meeting with this impressive list of individuals we had the opportunity to host these two visitors in an actual seminary setting on March 2, 1989.

They arrived at about nine-fifteen in the morning, and it was immediately apparent that we were dealing with two very gracious and kind gentlemen who really wanted to understand what we did in seminary. One thing that is unique about West is that it has a special education class that has five students in it, who have problems ranging from Down's syndrome to simple mental incapacitation. Probably the highest intelligence in the group is at about a six- or seven-year-old level, but the students are, as one would imagine, a sweet group of children. When our two guests arrived I invited them to visit this class, which was then in progress. We entered the back of the room while the teacher was in the midst of compiling a list of the good qualities of one of the students, who was having a birthday. The list included kindness and gentleness, and each of his classmates was making contributions. Then the teacher asked, "And who does Lonnie want to be like?"

A boy named Patrick, who has Down's syndrome, raised his hand and said, "Lonnie wants to be like J-e-s-u-s." I could see that that brought a twinkle to the eyes of our two guests. We then took the opportunity to introduce the children to them.

After the introductions the students were to have sung a birthday song to Lonnie, but they opted instead to sing "High on the Mountain Top," so they gathered around the piano. While the teacher played they sang to the best of their ability. Afterward, they wanted to sing "I Am a Child of God" for our visitors, and did so. We then told the class that we were going to have to leave to see some other parts of the seminary, but that we would listen as they sang the last song, which was "Because I Have Been Given Much." As they sang and we walked out of the classroom one of the visitors remarked to me, "We know that song. That's an old Baptist hymn." We were all quite touched to hear these children, who have so many special needs, singing "Because I have been given much, I too must give."

We next went into the back of my classroom, where the class was being taught by a substitute that period so I could be free to spend time with our two visitors. We watched for just a moment what was going on in the class and then went into my office. There the gentlemen began asking questions about the seminary program and about our beliefs as Latter-day Saints. They were especially interested in what we believed about the Lord's Supper, or the sacrament, since that had been the point of discussion in the class they had just visited.

As they continued to ask their questions, the host from the Church, Brother Briscoe, who was accompanying them throughout their itinerary in Salt Lake, turned to me and asked, "Brother Swanson, would you mind if these gentlemen talked to a couple of your students?"

I replied, "No, they're more than welcome to do so." One of them suggested that I choose a couple of students to bring into my office from the classroom, but I felt that it would be better if *I* didn't choose them, so that it could not possibly appear that I was "stacking the deck" in any way.

Within the class there was a wide range of students with every type of attitude, but all were basically good kids. (There was one girl in the class who had just enrolled and was in class for her very first day—that could have proven to be a rather interesting selection.) It was finally decided that Brother Briscoe would go into the classroom, randomly choose two students, and bring them in. He chose a boy and a girl whose names were Justin and Kim—a sophomore and a junior, respectively.

Here began one of the choice experiences I've had in my sixteen years with the Church Educational System. I moved my chair somewhat out of the way, so that the visitors would have full access to the students and so that the students wouldn't feel pressure to answer in any specific way. But I was, of course, able to listen to the conversation.

First of all our two guests introduced themselves, mentioning in the process who they were and that they represented a national organization concerned with religion and public education. Then they began asking the students some questions. For instance, they asked why they were taking seminary and why their friends took seminary. Did they feel that most of their friends were in seminary because they wanted to be there, or were they compelled by parental pressure?

Both of the students were very honest and responded that there were some in seminary who were there because their parents were making them take it, but that most who were enrolled loved the experience. Then both of these young people bore their testimonies of how important seminary was to them personally, and of how it helped them in their everyday living.

One of the visitors then asked them how the seminary students felt about the kids in the high school who weren't enrolled in seminary. Kim and Justin answered that they both had good friends who were not in seminary and mentioned that many non–Latter-day Saint students felt very comfortable coming over to the seminary to eat lunch, or just to visit between classes, or to come to the socials.

They were asked about where we receive our religious freedom and both mentioned the Constitution, which grants that freedom. Then one of our guests turned to Kim and asked if one church was more important than any other, in the United States. Both Kim and Justin expressed their feelings that one church was not more important than another in the history of our country, but that the Lord had given us free agency, the Constitution had guaranteed it, and the important thing was that everybody could worship as they wished. At that point these two wonderful, inspired young people bore their testimony of the gospel of Jesus Christ. First Justin talked about his deep love of the Savior, how he knew that when he prayed his Heavenly Father was listening, and that Jesus Christ cared for him enough to die for his sins. Then Kim talked about her personal struggle to gain a testimony. She related that there had been a time when she did not know for sure whether the Church was true, but that through prayer and scripture study and guidance from her parents she had finally received an answer to her prayers and had found, for herself, that the Church is true.

It was then time for our visitors to leave. The Spirit was very, very strong in that office, and as we sent the students back to class I had the opportunity to visit for just another moment or two with our guests. As they left, one of them commented that rather than being concerned that seminary violates the provision for separation of church from state, they couldn't understand why other churches didn't also make such a program available to their young people.

What profound teaching took place that morning! By watching two randomly chosen young people, as well as a class of so-called handicapped children, serve as the Lord's conduit, I learned that the Lord functions through each of us as the need arises to communicate truth to listening ears.

19

Traps

CORY BANGERTER

Teaching is a challenge, especially when it is a day-to-day experience. The challenge comes in having something fresh and captivating each class period for the students. On one occasion I was to teach a lesson on the dangers of sin and temptation. A friend of mine told me of an approach he used in such a situation, which involved the use of a number of actual traps. One was a small mousetrap, then a larger rattrap, followed by a muskrat trap, and finally a coyote trap. If possible, he would borrow a bear trap for effect. Then he would set the traps, talk about temptation and sin to his students, and one by one trigger each trap as the degree of sin went up. He would set off the mousetrap with his own finger, allowing himself to be slapped by it. Then he would use a ruler or a small stick to trigger the other traps, often breaking the stick in the process.

I was interested in presenting a similar lesson to my students. He agreed to loan me the needed traps and to explain how they worked. As arranged, one Saturday we met to discuss the proper approach to this lesson. He had brought

Cory Bangerter is the father of seven children and has been employed by the Church Educational System in a wide variety of assignments. He has been a seminary teacher and principal, has been involved in the writing of International Curriculum materials, and has been the Assistant Director of the Church's Literacy Program. He has served as the CES Director of Materials Production and an associate area director for Spain and Portugal. Brother Bangerter has also served on the Church Instructional Development Committee, in three bishoprics, as a high councilor, as a stake president's counselor, and as a mission president in Brazil.

along his four-year-old daughter to keep him company. We proceeded to set the traps, I learned how to trigger them, and in the process we talked and laughed about the fun of setting the traps and of relating them to various sins and temptations. We played with the trigger mechanisms, giggled, and challenged each other to test each trap. All of this was intended to create the excitement and thrill of danger involved with the perception of sin. At that point we sat down to discuss the proper strategy for making this presentation lively for the students.

Without our knowing it, his daughter had been watching from some distance. She, too, wanted to be a part of the fun, and when we sat down to talk she took the opportunity to see just how much fun the traps really were. We didn't notice her until her hand was raised over the coyote trap. As her hand began moving downward the two of us flew into action. My friend grabbed for his daughter and I dove with both hands for the trap. The timing couldn't have been more perfect. She had already triggered the trap, but at precisely that instant, I was able to stop the upward motion of the jaws and her father was able to extract her hand from danger. We then sat down, both of us terribly shaken by the nearness of tragedy.

We learned several lessons from the experience. First of all, it was a graphic demonstration of the devastating effects of the traps that Satan has set for us. That little girl could have been seriously injured and perhaps maimed by setting off the trap. Second, so many times people fall into traps in a very innocent way. The little girl had no ulterior motives or wicked desires. She was simply curious. Third, when we toy with the trigger mechanisms of sin, making light of them and pretending to have fun with danger, there are those around us, unknown to us, who may be listening and silently taking note of what they perceive to be proper behavior. After all, the girl must have reasoned, we were adults and both of us were her trusted friends. Why would we do anything that was wrong or that might bring harm to her?

The final lesson was taught, by a great father, who took advantage of a moment in which the window of his daughter's understanding was standing wide open. He took out a ruler, told her that it represented her hand, and triggered the coyote trap once more. Instantly the ruler was shattered in his hand. I will never forget the surprise and shock on the girl's face as she learned, through a vicarious experience, what happens when we play with sin.

20

Caring

EDWIN G. BROWN

One night my daughter, Rosanne, woke me at about one-thirty in the morning to tell me that a boy who was a good friend of hers had just had an extremely painful confrontation with his parents, and that he needed her. Marlin was a boy with quite a few challenges in his life, but Rosanne was attracted to him and seemed to be handling the situation well, so we had made him welcome in our home and had tried to show her we appreciated her point of view. On this occasion he and his parents had, apparently, really been going at it and he was threatening some rather drastic reactions to their argument. Rosanne felt that she really needed to be with him in order to calm him down and to offer perspective and prevent a possible tragedy. I agreed to get up and take her over to his house.

As we drove over I told her I was glad she was a caring person. I also said it was important to note the results of our caring and how it is received. We arrived at his house and I went to the door with her and told them that they had twenty

Ed Brown is the father of six children and co-owner and founder of the Highland Ridge Alcohol and Drug Abuse Treatment Center. He is a clinical psychologist, having received his doctorate from the University of Chicago, and continues a private practice while maintaining his responsibilities at Highland Ridge. He has been a member of the faculty at the University of Chicago, at BYU Hawaii, and at Latrobe University in Melbourne, Australia, and was dean of the Graduate School of Social Work at the University of Utah. He has served as a bishop, high councilor, and ward mission leader, and is currently the Gospel Doctrine class teacher in his ward.

minutes to talk. Then Rosanne would have to go home and get back to bed. They used all of the time.

On the way home Rosanne remarked that she just couldn't believe she had a dad who would get up in the middle of the night, drive his daughter to a friend's house, sit in the car for twenty minutes, and then drive her home—all without grumbling or laying some guilt trip on her. She commented further that she did not believe that a single one of her friends had a dad who would do that. She was deeply touched. More important, our ride and visit together had created an atmosphere of genuine consideration and analysis of the situation. There were no barriers of resentment to be overcome and she could observe the circumstances objectively. The payoff came about three months later.

Things had gotten worse for Marlin, and one day I asked Rosanne how he was doing. She said that he wasn't doing very well and that the talking and persuading she was doing were being mostly ignored. I asked her to recall all the concern and pain she had felt for Marlin the night we had gone to his house. She said it had been very uncomfortable. I asked her how Marlin had been acting since then. She said he was not being very responsible—that he was breaking all the rules, going out with the kids and using drugs, and then acting as though nothing had happened.

I asked how much benefit he was getting from her caring. She replied that he had been ignoring it—so she had backed off. She realized that *he* had to do the work of changing his life, and that she couldn't do it for him. Her caring, she said, was being taken advantage of. She was the one who was doing all the hurting and feeling, while Marlin continued to do as he pleased, with no apparent intention to change. Also, he was not in tune with her concerns or the pain she felt when he got into trouble.

My daughter had learned a valuable lesson in human relations. Simply stated, it is that giving and being there for another are wonderful gifts that can help others in times of need. However, these gifts can be taken advantage of and become enabling behaviors that keep the other person from changing and experiencing the natural consequences of his choices. She also came to realize that this kind of interaction in a relationship can actually be harmful to the helping friend, if the one who helps is the only one who does any giving. By trying to do the work that only the other person can do, this person experiences stress and pain that the receiving person completely disregards.

Life's lessons are learned by understanding our experiences. That late-night ride with my daughter to visit a troubled friend taught her how to respect herself and still be a caring person.

21

I Guess He Must Be Human

ROBERT L. MILLET

I have come to appreciate that some of the most effective teaching in the Church is done outside the formal classroom setting. Sometimes the questions that are asked and answered, the unanticipated insight that is gained, the applications that are made, the love that is expressed, and the resolve and commitment that are formed outside of classes are far more lasting and valuable than what goes on during the designated class period.

This lesson was brought home to me most forcefully some years ago when I was teaching seminary. My fourth period class was a lively and active group, but a good bunch of kids. We enjoyed each other a great deal and had some marvelous experiences in studying the Old Testament together. There was, however, one fly in the ointment—a young man we'll call Larry who took an immediate dislike to me as soon as school started and simply refused to feel otherwise.

Bob Millet is the father of six children and was employed by LDS Social Services before turning to the Church Educational System. He has been a seminary teacher, an institute instructor, and a teaching support consultant. Employed by Brigham Young University as an associate professor, he is currently the chairman of the Department of Ancient Scripture. He is the author and/or editor of numerous books and articles on LDS history and doctrine. Brother Millet has been a bishop, a high councilor, and a stake president's counselor, and has served as a temple worker. In addition he has served on the General Church Curriculum Committee and on the Church Materials Evaluation Committee.

I would come into the room a little early each morning only to find sarcastic and sometimes rather vulgar messages on the chalkboard, always addressed to me. And Larry made no effort to hide his hatred—he was always courteous enough to sign the little beauties. He had a most interesting way, in class, of disrupting things: he would clear his throat or cough loudly just at the moment when I was trying to make an important point, or just at the time when a very touching line in a story was being reached. His timing was perfect. He was quite creative as well, and occasionally resorted to pushing desks over at crucial times, thereby destroying the teaching moment and causing snickering and laughter among the other students. Whenever I attempted to talk with him after class he was spiteful and nasty with me, and he never hesitated to assure me that I was wasting his and the other kids' time. Part of the problem was that he was a natural leader—a great athlete, as well as a high school class officer—and many of his peers were, unfortunately, prone to follow his actions and attitudes.

I prayed earnestly for the Lord's help, especially desiring that my feeling of affection for him might grow and that he might be able to feel both my love and the truthfulness of the message in class. I don't know why, but I simply couldn't dislike the little cuss! But the problem persisted for a number of weeks, and I soon began to observe that some of my better and more well-behaved students were starting to march to the beat of his dissident drum.

One afternoon a group of the seminary faculty members went to a nearby university gym to play basketball. After we had been running up and down the court for about an hour, and at the point where a number of us who hadn't exercised seriously for a year were ready for coronary care, I noticed my classroom challenge standing at the other end of the gymnasium. I waved to him, but he didn't respond, other than to smirk. He simply moved outside the gym and watched from a distance, being careful not to be seen.

The next day in class I noticed that Larry was unusually quiet. I wondered if perhaps he had a cold or a sore throat, since he hadn't taken the occasion to clear his throat or cough through the whole lesson. He approached me after class and said, rather timidly, "You're pretty good."

I answered, "Excuse me?"

"You're pretty good," he said again, "at basketball, I mean. I saw you playing yesterday and you shoot really well."

I hemmed and hawed and apologized for the fact that I hadn't played any serious ball for ten years or more. He gave me a half-smile as he left and quietly made his way down the stairs. What happened thereafter was remarkable: Larry took part in class, made constructive and thoughtful contributions to our discussion, threatened to beat up anyone who was disruptive, and began to spend long hours chatting with me after class about the gospel. He became a delight to be around. He later served as a seminary officer as well as high school student-body president.

I have pondered over the abrupt and unusual manner in which Larry's attitude toward me and toward seminary changed; it seems that he must have seen me in a different light on the basketball court. I suppose he pictured me, previously, as spending much of my leisure time in cloistered halls and in monastic fashion poring over ancient and dusty manuscripts. I was, therefore, attempting to guide him from a point of view that had nothing to do with him. In the space of a few moments he had learned that my outlook was not what he had supposed it to be. Suddenly having that perspective altered, he seemed to say, "Well, what do you know—he must be human too." The messenger was given a second chance, as was the message. Bars were dropped. Prejudices were removed. Friendship was established, and a soul was refocused on the things of greatest worth.

Truly God does move in mysterious ways. The work of conversion is the work of the Holy Ghost. The person called to deliver the lesson can study and search and ponder and pray; he or she can testify and love and seek earnestly to provide a setting and an environment for gospel study. But the real instructor, the timeless and timely teacher, is the Holy Ghost. He knows the hearts and minds and needs of individuals. He is the personal tutor, the member of the Godhead designated to create a readiness and a receptiveness for lasting learning. He may choose to do so in the unlikely confines of a gymnasium. We do not know his methods or his timing. We cannot know. But once he has provided the sons and daughters of God with a new vision, with an elevated perspective, nothing else is ever quite the same.

22

The Door Begins to Open

JEAN ASAY

One year, as I was teaching ninth grade seminary, I taught a boy who often missed class and who came in late nearly every time he did come. His assigned seat was in the front of the class and I welcomed the opportunity to have him close enough to be able to encourage him to participate. He admitted that he was there only because his parents insisted that he come, that he would really rather be with his friends. As I asked him more about his friends and his family he admitted he was more comfortable with his friends because they didn't judge him and he felt accepted by them. I remembered this conversation during the following weeks as I noticed changes in his behavior and attitude. Sometimes he would speak out belligerently, refuse to participate in any way, and respond with anger at any attempt I made to communicate with him.

I observed him very closely and talked with him briefly during and after class on several occasions. After doing so for a number of weeks, I concluded that he was coming to class "stoned" (to use his word) more often than not.

After much thought and prayer, I asked him to stay after class to visit with me. I prayed that I would find the right words and that he would be receptive. I was prompted to ask

Jean Asay, the mother of four children, played a key role in the piloting of the Outreach Program in the Salt Lake City area and for a number of years was a volunteer with LDS Social Services. She has served in several Young Women and Relief Society presidencies. A former missionary to the West Central States, Sister Asay is frequently called on to do workshops on scripture study and, for some years, has been employed by the Church Educational System, in both a teaching and a secretarial capacity.

him a question and I surprised both myself and him when the first thing I said was, "How long do you plan to come to class in this condition?"

He responded with, "What do you mean?"

Using his name I replied that while I didn't know for sure what he was using, I did know that he was coming to class "stoned" most of the time.

Not in an unkind way, he smiled and said he was surprised I knew the right word for his condition. But he did not deny it, and because feelings of trust and caring were felt between us, and because the prayer of my heart was heard, we talked together openly and honestly for a long time. This hour did not magically solve his problems, but it opened the door for a relationship that offered encouragement and acceptance and support as he gradually regained control of his life.

Before he left that day, he looked straight into my eyes, maybe for the first time, and said, "Not one teacher in any of my other classes has asked me about coming to class 'stoned.' You are the only one."

How grateful I was that, through the assistance of the Spirit, a moment of impact had been established and I had been able to take advantage of it to the ongoing benefit of this young man.

23

Eternal Instruction

ED J. PINEGAR

As a leader of young missionaries for four years I had struggled with the question of motivation. I had searched scripture, used reasoning and logic, and pleaded with my Heavenly Father for insight. I felt that in order to get to the heart of productivity in missionaries and to offer them a key to the conversion process I needed the answer to a question: What is the beginning—the stepping off place—of righteous desire? I felt that if I could get a handle on that, if I could get to the very seeds of desiring righteousness, I could help missionaries and investigators to know how to begin.

At 4:00 A.M. on December 25, 1988, I was awakened by a direct response from the heavens to my four-year search. Apparently Heavenly Father had some growing for me to do and so had allowed me to pursue the answer to my question and to struggle for all those months. But at that time, as he always does, he began to provide the reward for the price I had been paying in this pursuit. This time the answer wasn't found in a witness of the Spirit to a passage of scripture or in the words of a modern prophet. It was one of those occasions when the Spirit communicated directly and tangibly to another spirit

Ed Pinegar, the father of eight children, has a degree in dentistry from the University of Southern California and practiced in that profession for many years until Church service occupied his time fully. He has recently been released as the president of the Missionary Training Center in Provo, Utah, prior to which call he was the president of the England London South Mission. Earlier, he took enough time from his practice to teach seminary and to teach religion at BYU part-time. He has been a bishop, has served on the Young Men general board, and is the author of three books.

through no medium but Himself. He impressed a comprehension indelibly on my mind and in my heart. I got up immediately and wrote it down: "Recognizing the goodness of God puts the knowledge that he loves us into our hearts. That great moment then produces the fruit of gratitude. Upon feeling grateful, our desires to please him increase and righteous behavior can be the result. Therefore, *gratitude* is the beginning of all righteous desire."

In those few moments, in the stillness which encourages such communications, Spirit had spoken to spirit and had conveyed the eternal truth for which I had become eligible. I had been instructed from on high in one of the great teaching moments of my life.

24

Laughing

CAROL BRANDT

As a young mother I was faced, one Sabbath morning, with a dilemma. My son, David, had been asked to present his first talk in church and was getting cold feet. As we sat together on the stand, he turned to me and said, "Mommy, what if they laugh at me?"

Sensing I was hearing a very real concern, and wanting to take advantage of a pivotal moment, I thought to myself that if I agreed with him that his listeners might, in fact, laugh at him (which I knew to be a genuine possibility), then he probably wouldn't get up to give the talk. On the other hand, I also realized that if I assured him that they wouldn't laugh at him and then they did, he might never muster the courage to give another talk.

As I hovered in one of those instantaneous eternities I was prompted to suggest a third possibility. I said, "Oh, I hope they do—because that will mean you are making them happy." His fear having been dispelled, he approached the stand confidently and gave the talk. His courage to stand and speak to audiences has not faltered since then.

Carol Brandt is the mother of eight children. She has been to Israel and the Middle East eight times, seven of them in the capacity of tour co-leader. Sister Brandt has served on the Church Family Home Evening Resource Committee and the Church Teaching Resource Committee and is currently a member of the Church Curriculum Research Committee.

25

Clean Slate

MACK GRIFFITH

Some years ago I had a young man in one of my seminary classes who was only there to please his girlfriend. This sweet young lady was determined to have him gain a testimony, go on a mission, and then take her to the temple. Well, we didn't have much success in getting his attention, and for the most part he spent his energy on homework from his other classes. However, there were times when his head would come up from his schoolbooks and he would listen intently for a time— only to return to the demands of finishing his history or English assignments. This went on for the better part of a semester, although we did see some progress. He began to listen a little more often and even asked some questions on occasion.

Then one day in my preparation I came across Elder Bruce R. McConkie's commentary on James 5:20, which says, ". . . he which converteth the sinner . . . shall hide a multitude of sins." Elder McConkie wrote that, "Those who preach the gospel and bring souls into the kingdom . . . [are] rewarded" by being "freed from [their] own sins." (*Doctrinal New Testament Commentary*, vol. 3 [Salt Lake City: Bookcraft, 1973], p. 279.) I had often wondered how a person could repent of the many sins that had been committed and then forgotten. Also, my students often asked how they could

Mack Griffith is the father of five children and has been employed by the Church Educational System for twenty-four years as a seminary instructor and principal. He has served as a bishop and a stake president's counselor.

be assured that they were forgiven of the sins of which they had repented. Here was an exciting doctrine which pointed out that if you repent and bear testimony through missionary work you can be assured that your sins are forgiven. I thought of the many young people I knew who were carrying around a burden of sins for which they had repented but for which they had not extended to themselves forgiveness. Now I had found a doctrine that could give them hope. I was excited. I searched to see if others had taught the same principle. I found that they had and that the Doctrine and Covenants, in fact, contained the principle. President Kimball had so taught. I couldn't wait to get into the classroom.

There were two things that the class and I knew about our friend who was reluctantly joining us for the sake of his girlfriend. He loved his car and, quite obviously, he loved the girl. I was determined to test the depth of his feelings.

The discussion began with the question, "Wouldn't it be nice to have a clean slate—to have all sins eliminated?" The class readily agreed that it would. I suggested that I had discovered a promise from the Lord in the scriptures concerning how to achieve just that state of cleanness—which thing I had never supposed. I explained that I had just come across this concept the night before and that I wanted to share it with them. Everyone was intent and waiting expectantly. I called our reluctant class member by his first name and said, "What would you give to have a clean slate?"

He responded immediately and I sensed his geniune sincerity. "I would give anything."

"Would you give your car?" The class listened eagerly.

"Yes," he responded emphatically and without hesitation. The next question was almost unfair.

"Would you give up your girlfriend?"

He almost answered, but hesitated and looked at her across the aisle. "What do I have to do?"

"You have to give up your girlfriend for two years."

It sunk in immediately. "Go on a mission?"

"Yes. Let's look at some scriptures."

I thought he was going to rip the cover off the book in order to get to the verses that were written on the board. I asked him to read them for us. I wish I had the words to describe the look on his face. There, on the young man's face, was the reward—the paycheck—for my teaching. If that return comes once a year, or even every ten years, the effort is worth the struggle. The lesson continued but that wonderful young man, who was entering a transition, couldn't take his eyes off those scriptures. He read them over and over and over again.

His interest in seminary and in the Church took an incredible leap during the next few months. The conclusion of the matter smacks of fiction, and yet it is true. He gained a testimony, went on his mission, and married the girl in the temple when he got home. This is the course he was turned to in a moment when Spirit and scripture worked together to profoundly influence his life.

26

Unimpressed

BRAD ROCK

The year that Richie Webb was a freshman at Brigham Young University there was a sportswriter who traveled with the basketball team who was not a Latter-day Saint. He was a chain-smoker and was just a bit out of sync with the atmosphere of the B.Y.U. setting. One day on an airplane the writer approached me, laughing, and said, "That Richie Webb, he was reading the Book of Mormon and trying to get me to read it. He doesn't know how all you guys, all these years, have been trying to convert me."

I laughed with him, but inwardly was deeply impressed that a freshman, in these intimidating surroundings, was trying to get the spiritual attention of this rather hardened, fifty-two-year-old man. He didn't stop to consider the odds or the circumstances—he just forged ahead, willing to let the consequences follow. I'm not sure whether the old sportswriter learned anything about the gospel of Jesus Christ on that occasion, but I did.

Brad Rock is the father of five children and is currently employed as a sportswriter for the Deseret News *in Salt Lake City. Prior to his present employment he held the same position with the* Gallup Independent *in Gallup, New Mexico. He has served for several years as the Young Men president in his ward and is currently a counselor to the stake Young Men president.*

27

In Spite of Himself

CAMILLE FRONK

Just one week into the school year a freshman boy named Kyle handed me a yellow paper from the high school informing me that he was transferring out of seventh period seminary to play football. I was disappointed in his choice, but saw no alternative other than to sign the paper and to invite him to come back to visit when he tired of football

Imagine my surprise when, a month and a half later, Kyle's mother came to the scheduled parent-teacher conferences to see how her son was doing in seminary. Thinking she had forgotten the decision I assumed that she had agreed to weeks before, I briefly reminded her that her son played football during seventh period. Her look of complete shock gave me my first clue that Kyle had outsmarted the administration his first week in high school.

After convincing each other that we were both talking about the same boy, she assured me that Kyle would be back in my seventh period seminary class the following Monday. I cringed as I envisioned the delightful discussion Kyle would have with his mother later that evening, then panicked when I realized that I would be expected to teach him the joys of righteous living starting on Monday.

Camille Fronk graduated from Utah State University with a bachelor's degree and holds a master's degree from Brigham Young University in Near Eastern Studies. She was employed by the Church Educational System for eight years as a seminary teacher and is now the dean of students at LDS Business College. She has served as a Relief Society president and a Young Women president, has held many teaching positions, and is currently serving as a member of the Young Women general board.

True to his mother's vow, Kyle was back the following Monday, and with something other than joy and gladness showing in his countenance. Rather, he plopped down at a desk and brought his head to rest securely on it in one single movement. Without saying a word, he had let me know that he had not appreciated my revealing his secret and that he longed to be far from the confining seminary walls.

During the weeks since Kyle had transferred out of class, it had developed into a close-knit, inquisitive group of budding gospel scholars. No matter what the topic, they could bring the lesson to apply directly to their personal lives just by their specific, sincere questions.

Kyle was coming to class now every day (whatever Mom threatened had definitely worked!) and I had hopes that maybe the kind of environment the class presented would get him at least a little enthused. But it wasn't to be so simple.

I marveled frequently that he could stay so distant and apathetic through some of our discussions, which were, in fact, anything but passive. On occasion, he would raise his head and glare at a student who had just asked a question, as if to say, "I can't believe I'm in the same class as this bunch of goons."

I wasn't the only one who was trying to get a ray of sunshine to peek through Kyle's gloomy front. The class members consistently invited him to help with devotionals, to participate in scripture competition, or just to talk before class started. With few exceptions, he remained aloof.

The situation improved only slightly during the course of the year. The only really positive thing I could report was that he attended regularly.

Near the end of the school year we held a seminary-wide testimony meeting at which, during each period of the day, the students all met together in order to express to each other their feelings about the part the gospel played in their lives. In most cases, the seniors were the enthusiastic participants and the freshmen were quite amazed that people would actually subject themselves to such torture. The ninth grade boys usually sat on the back row, their chairs propped back against the wall, trying to hold in the laughter when someone got emotional.

About three-fourths of the way through the meeting in seventh period, I saw Kyle stand up and start walking toward the front. My first thought was that he was going to leave because it was all too gushy. But he walked all the way to the microphone, causing his fellow freshmen to come suddenly forward on their chairs, their jaws gaping open. I must admit that my jaw dropped too. The expression on Kyle's face was a new one to me and I wondered what he would say. Was there any way it could possibly be appropriate for this setting?

He began by relating his deception of his mother the preceding fall, and how, when he was found out, he had to return to seminary. He explained his desire to let everyone know that he was there only because he had no other choice, and that he was not interested in the Church at all.

He said further, "I kept my head down on the desk most of the time. I figured that that way no one would mistake me for a 'Bible Boy.' However, keeping my head down kept me from seeing, but I couldn't stop myself from hearing." He said he began listening to some of the other students' questions and admitted to himself that he had wondered some of the same things. He listened for answers, which many times sparked other questions in his mind. He waited for other class members to ask the questions that were forming in his own mind, but they rarely did. He often came back the next day hoping to have his questions asked, only to leave disappointed. Once, he said, he almost raised his hand to ask a question, but caught himself just in time. What would people think?

When he couldn't stand it any longer Kyle went home and asked his dad, who was considered less active in the Church at the time. His dad's response rather surprised Kyle. "I've wondered that myself," he said. "Let's see if we can find an answer." They first looked in the few Church books they had at home, and when those didn't satisfy them, father and son went to the public library to check out other books.

At this point in the sharing of his testimony, Kyle started fighting back tears. "I've never talked to my dad like I have since we started looking for answers together. It was great! I began to come to seminary so that I could get more questions to take home to ask Dad. My dad goes to church with us now. We sit together as a family. I never knew it could be so great. Never again will I fight against the Church. It's brought our family together."

That summer Kyle's family was sealed together in the Jordan River Temple. The following fall Kyle was called as the president of his seminary class. And three years later his parents were in the Assembly Hall on Temple Square to see him graduate from seminary.

28

Modern Corianton

MICHAEL SHURTLEFF

Her name was Kim. As a sophomore in high school she fell in love with an older boy. Against the advice of all who counseled her, she married him and left school.

I first received Kim's name in the early fall. As a teacher in the alternative program of the Department of Seminaries and Institutes it wasn't unusual to hear some pretty heart-rending stories. Kim's topped them all. Her husband had involved her in all forms of immorality, drug abuse, and drug addiction and dealing. She had taken a roller coaster ride through life and had ended up at the bottom. It took the arrest and imprisonment of her husband, their subsequent divorce, and her confinement in a drug treatment program to bring her back to her home and to our program.

When I first met Kim she was a hard case. Although she was only eighteen years old, her face reflected many years of troubled living. Our first class together was far from successful. It ended with my leaving a notebook and a copy of the Book of Mormon, together with instructions to read a few passages and record her feelings.

The next week was interesting. Following a word of prayer, she read to me what she had written: "Nephi's brothers tie him up and beat him with sticks." After a few minutes

Mike Shurtleff is the father of six children and is currently serving as a bishop. He has been employed by the Church Educational System for eight years, where he was previously the principal of the Park City Seminary and is presently the principal of the Jordan Alternative Seminary. Active in community affairs, he has served as the chairman of his mass meeting block area and as a member of the Cottonwood Creek Community Council.

of discussion I left her, with instructions to continue reading and writing her feelings. I encouraged her to pray, but she didn't. The next week went much like the first, as did subsequent weeks. Progress was not being made very quickly.

As I drove up to Kim's house after Christmas vacation, I felt some apprehension. In the past, when I had not seen her for a few weeks little or no progress had been made. I said a silent prayer for help and went up to the door and knocked. As I entered there was something different about the atmosphere in her home. It was hard to put my finger on what it was, but it was a new kind of feeling.

We began with prayer and then Kim opened her notebook and began to tell me about her most recent experience. She recounted her reading of Alma's counsel to his son Corianton. She told me that, as she was reading, she recollected all of her own past sins. She found herself on her knees by her bed and began pouring out her heart in prayer. She had a similar experience to that which Alma had had himself, earlier in his life.

Our tears flowed freely as she shared these sacred moments with me. We turned to Abinadi's discourse on the Savior and the Atonement, which he delivered before King Noah. Again tears flowed as the Spirit bore testimony of the truth of what we had been studying. We learned together for nearly two hours, but it seemed like minutes. We were both taught by the scriptures and by the Spirit that emanates so powerfully from them.

The classes that followed built from that session, and Kim began to take the first steps back toward her former self. She has since completed high school and is now preparing to serve a mission.

That morning I was taught, along with Kim, that when the Spirit combines with scripture to instruct, some of our most profound learning takes place.

29

Accountability and the Spirit

F. GERALD THOMPSON

A number of years ago it fell my lot to have a fifth-period seminary class with a very interesting mix of students. The high school student-body president and vice-president were members of the class, as were several very beautiful young women, who were among the most popular in the school. There were two or three very shy, quiet girls as well, along with some big, boisterous football players. My oldest son also was in the class. I knew, as they entered the room that very first day, that it was bound to be my most severe test to date as a seminary teacher. How could I mold this diverse group of young people into a unified, harmonious class? How could I direct their varied interests and talents into a single focus of studying the gospel?

Days passed and my worst fears were realized. This was a rowdy group. One huge young man, in particular, was especially vocal as he entered the room each day. He seemed to take great delight in creating a lot of noise and in using obnoxious language. Try as I might to find his good side and to win him over, I could not do it.

One day, as we started the devotional, in he came in his blustering way, using a selection of his usual profane words. This was it! I had had enough. How dare he violate the class-

Jerry Thompson is the father of six children and was a pharmacist for the first twenty-five years of his professional life. He is currently employed as a seminary principal and has been with the Church Educational System for nineteen years. Brother Thompson has served on two high councils and in two bishoprics.

room and offend the sensitive ears of these young girls with his rudeness and profanity!

I believe the Spirit knows when God's sons and daughters are teachable, even when we don't, and that the Spirit therefore moves us to words and actions in their behalf—words and actions which we might not have chosen on our own. I now believe that this was such an occasion.

I raised my voice to a level equal to his and heard myself say: "Brian! Who do you think you are that you can come in here and conduct yourself in this manner? Now sit down and act as if someone has taught you some manners!"

There was sudden silence in the room and a look of surprise on Brian's face. He sat down and didn't say another word. His friends followed his example and were attentive during the rest of the hour. Several days passed without another incident.

As this new course became a pattern, I began to have thoughts of Brian as the class president. I quickly dismissed these thoughts, wondering how such a ridiculous idea had ever entered into my mind. But the feeling kept returning, and one evening I paid a visit to Brian's home, where I met his family and explained why I had come.

Brian was an outstanding president. He changed the direction of the class. It became a custom for him to call on someone to share his or her testimony once or twice a week as part of the devotional. I heard my own son bear his testimony for the very first time in that fifth-period class. A spiritual dimension developed there that I shall not forget.

Brian became a great advocate of seminary and bore his own testimony often in his ward, telling how he set out at first to destroy a seminary class but was moved by the Spirit as he was called to account for his conduct. The divine instruction he received in those moments of reflection had changed his life and had significantly influenced an entire class of his peers.

30

For I Am Not Ashamed

GREG DOWNS

Not long ago a good friend of mine, whom we'll call Steve, related to me an experience that had broadened his perspective beyond description. His father had developed a kidney disease known as nephritis, which eventually proved fatal. The disease had reduced a once strong, well-built man to well under one hundred pounds. He became quite frail, and immediately prior to his death his features and general appearance had become greatly altered.

Two weeks before Steve's father died, the two of them had gone to the local market to do some grocery shopping. As they emerged from the store, both carrying shopping bags, Steve quickened his pace a little as they hurried to their parked car. But as he turned to say something to his father, Steve was startled to discover that his father wasn't beside him anymore. He was still standing back at the store's main entrance, staring down at the pavement, both bags sitting on the ground beside him. Steve ran back to his father's side and, gently raising his head, saw tears running down his cheeks. When Steve asked his father what the matter was, his father replied, "Son, are you ashamed to walk with me?"

Steve said to me that he had never before experienced pain of this kind or of this magnitude. Through his own tears

Greg Downs is the father of five children and has been employed as an instructor and principal in the Church Educational System for fifteen years. He holds a bachelor's degree from Weber State University and a master's degree from Brigham Young University, and has been a bishop and a high councilor. Brother Downs has contributed many hours to Little League baseball and basketball.

he assured his father that he was in no way ashamed to walk with him, no matter what the disease had done to his appearance, and that he loved him now as much as he always had. Oblivious to a now-curious group of onlookers, they embraced each other and shed tears of endearment, grateful for the bond that existed between them.

Two weeks later, following the funeral, Steve's mind was turned again to those moments outside the grocery store. The Spirit suggested to him a parallel between the feelings his father had had, when he thought that his son was ashamed to be seen with him, and the feelings his Savior must have when Steve seemed ashamed to be identified with him. He reflected on the deep pain that he had experienced himself, when he realized what pain he had caused his father, and resolved to be more consistently aware of staying beside the Savior and not allowing himself to drift from His side. He felt a clearer commitment to prevent further pain to the Brother he loved even more than he loved his father.

31

A Sign of Love

RICHARD L. PORTER

Our eight-year-old son Michael had received an invitation to go to the Saturday birthday party of a school friend. The party had been the subject of conversation in class most of the week, and big plans were laid. When Mike's out-of-town friend, Frank, came in for a four-day visit, it only increased the excitement around our house. Mike seemed to have everything he could want going for him. That's when Frank announced that on Saturday he was throwing a huge party at his grandmother's ranch. There would be baseball and other games, plenty of food, and even horseback riding. It was the ideal boys' party—at least from our point of view as parents. For Michael, however, it was a very un-ideal dilemma.

We felt bad, of course, that he would have to turn down one of the invitations. But to us there seemed little difficulty in deciding which party to attend. Although the other invitation had been extended first, Mike would not see Frank again for another year or more; and he would see the other boy nearly every day. Mike's brother Rob had also been invited to Frank's party, but he had already said that he didn't want to go unless Mike did. So if Mike refused Frank's invitation, it

Richard Porter is the father of eight children and has been employed by the Church Educational System as a seminary instructor and principal. He has been the teaching support consultant for the northern portion of the Salt Lake Valley seminaries and, currently, for the Southern Arizona seminaries. He is also concurrently the pre-service director (training of new seminary teachers) for the Southern Arizona area. Brother Porter is also a consultant with Interstate Trucking of Salt Lake City, Utah. He has served as a bishop and a high councilor.

was a refusal for two. We also assumed that Mike would personally rather go to the party where he could ride horses, but that he might feel hesitant to say no to the first invitation. So we shared our feelings with him, and assured him that his schoolfriend would understand.

That's why we were so surprised when Mike came and told us he couldn't make up his mind. He didn't want to hurt the feelings of either friend, and that was part of the struggle. But beyond that, he really wanted to go to the birthday party and skip Frank's. And yet he was very aware of the counsel that we had given him. In fact, by this time we had come to feel that it was important for Mike to go to Frank's party for several reasons: because Frank would be leaving for a year; because Rob was also invited; and because there were only a very few special friends invited to Frank's party, and a small mob to the other. We reasoned with Mike, certain that he really wanted to go to Frank's party but felt obligated to accept the first invitation.

Around ten in the morning Mike came to my office, tears of frustration welling in his eyes. He was still totally uncertain what was right. He wanted to go to the birthday party . . . "sort of." And he *did* want to ride the horses . . . "sort of."

"Mike," I said, "have you prayed about it?"

"No," he answered. "Should I pray about a party?"

I explained that Heavenly Father is willing to help us in everything, if we will just trust him enough to ask. I urged him to try it.

He was back in about ten minutes. "Dad, how do I know if Heavenly Father has answered me?"

I realized then that this was one of those times that require a father's full attention. I struggled for the right answer. He seemed so young to understand something that adults ask about all the time. Normally, I would turn to Doctrine and Covenants 9:7–9, but Mike was only eight years old. However, unable to think of any other way to answer, I plunged in, keeping my answer as simple as possible. I suggested that he make the best decision he could, then tell Heavenly Father what it was. Then he could ask Heavenly Father if it was the right decision.

"Mike, if it is right, then you will feel a special warm, good feeling inside, and you will feel excited to do what you have decided. If it is wrong you will still feel that sick feeling in your stomach, and you will still wonder if it is right. You will still be confused.''

With full faith that it would work, he returned to his room. I sent up a silent prayer that Heavenly Father would teach him, as the scriptures say. I wanted Heavenly Father to know how important this was to both Mike and me. The next few minutes seemed long, but when Mike came running up the stairs, I knew he felt good.

"Dad, I know which party I'm going to! I told Heavenly Father that I would go to the birthday party, and I feel really good, and excited about it, just like you said I would if it was right.''

For my part, I was surprised. We had felt so certain that the right thing was for him to go to Frank's party that I fully expected Heavenly Father would tell him that. In other words, I felt he had received the wrong answer. But I did not want in any way to shake his faith in the process he had just learned.

"Mike, I'm glad Heavenly Father answered your prayer. I knew he would. I know he is very pleased that you would trust him in that way.''

Then Mike drew a little closer and said, "Dad, I'm not sure that I felt that special feeling you said I would.''

I wanted so much to answer the right way. Maybe he had felt the feeling, but just didn't recognize it. "Mike, perhaps sometimes just the excited, happy feeling comes, and that is our answer. You don't feel frustrated and confused anymore, do you?''

He shook his head no. But the Spirit would not let me stop with that. "Mike, maybe you should pray one more time. Only this time, tell Heavenly Father that you are going to go to Frank's party, and ask him if that is right.''

All sorts of thoughts ran through my mind while I waited for Mike to come back upstairs. Foremost was the thought that there really are some times when it makes no real difference which decision we make. Neither carries eternal significance, and Heavenly Father really doesn't care which we do. We must learn sometimes to struggle and find answers on our own. Surely, which party for an eight-year-old to attend is that kind of decision. And yet, it seemed such a good chance for Mike to learn an important truth about his relationship with his Father in Heaven. Some minutes later, Mike returned.

"Dad," he began, "I'm going to Frank's party at the ranch. I did what you said, and while I was praying, I felt a strange feeling in my body. I felt warm all over. And now I really do feel excited about going to Frank's party."

I gave him a hug, told him how much I loved him, and suggested that he go thank Heavenly Father for helping him. He ran from my office to offer that prayer, and then to call Frank and his other friend. I closed my door, overwhelmed by the "strange feeling" in my own body, and by feeling "warm all over." Then I knelt to thank Heavenly Father for loving his son—our son—so much, and for caring about even the smallest things that sometimes overwhelm us.

32

Individual Benefits in Searching the Scriptures

ROBERT J. MATTHEWS

Although everyone in our classes of religion is expected to read the same chapters from the scriptures, the benefit that comes to each person varies with his needs and diligence. The scriptures are springs of "living water," and each person can come and drink as he or she has need. Often the teacher has a particular goal of a concept or an objective to be obtained by the students. While this is generally necessary to giving order, system, and progression to the class experience, the difficulty lies in the fact that the objective is often "thought up" and developed by the teacher. Sometimes the students may have other needs, and there may be information in a given passage other than that which the teacher has himself seen or realized. Every person should read the scriptures for himself, so that each can draw from the word of the Lord that which is needed at the time.

This point was emphasized to me one day at the conclusion of a Pearl of Great Price course that I had been teaching,

Robert Matthews has been the chairman of the Department of Ancient Scripture within the College of Religion at Brigham Young University and served for many years as the dean of that college. He was recently released to pursue more actively his responsibilities as one of the senior editors of the Encyclopedia of Mormonism. *He has been employed as an instructor in the seminaries and institutes of religion and has been a curriculum writer, researcher, and editor for the Church Educational System. Brother Matthews has been a stake president and a stake patriarch and has served as a member of the Church's Adult Correlation Review Committee and of the Scriptures Publications Committee. He is the author of several books and numerous articles on gospel topics and is the recognized authority on the history and contribution of the Joseph Smith Translation of the Bible.*

when I asked whether anyone wished to express what they had learned or how the course had benefited them. I recall one person enthusiastically praising what the Pearl of Great Price had taught him about Moses—"Moses the Magnificent" were his exact words. Another was happy to have learned more about Abraham through the Pearl of Great Price than is possible through other scriptures.

There were several other such expressions, all of which were in keeping with the stated objectives of the class. After nearly everyone had left the room, one student said he would like to tell me what had benefited him the most from the book of Abraham. He said it was meaningful to him to see "that Abraham made it in spite of having a father who was inactive in the Church."

I was surprised at what he told me, but I saw at once that he had gained something that he needed and which was precious and spiritual to him, but which was not a point of emphasis in the lesson plans or lectures. His point was real and important and scriptural, but it would have been missed entirely if the student had not been reading for himself. He drank from the well of living water and the Spirit touched him as he read. The Spirit knew his needs and had highlighted that aspect of the passage as he read.

Each year while teaching the Book of Mormon, when we have finished the book of Alma I ask the students what it was they valued most, or what meant the most to them, in Alma. There are always a variety of answers, but the most frequent one is that they enjoyed the chapters in which Alma gave fatherly advice to his sons. In these young students' minds these chapters outperform the excitement of the wars, the information on doctrine, and the wonderful missionary experiences. Each person drinks as he or she has thirst.

33

To Whom Will You Listen?

STEWART GLAZIER

Turning off the paved road, my eyes caught a glimpse of what later became my refiner's fire. Instead of tall, shady trees, we were greeted by two- to three-foot-high saplings that had recently budded. Instead of well-cared-for ground, it was sunbaked and hard. Where the water did touch the thirsty field, weeds were so abundant that it was difficult to distinguish between them and the young citrus trees. I thought again of the dollar an hour I had come to this place to earn, and wondered if it was really worth the effort it would demand.

The only thing that eased my dusty vision was the refreshing Arizona canal which ran nearby, giving its lifeblood to the thirsty crops. Beside the canal was a small grove of mesquite trees, under which stretched an army cot that had seen better days and which was evidently used during the heat of the day.

"This is it, boys. Come here, and I'll explain what I want you to do." The voice belonged to Judge Struckmeyer, one of Arizona's supreme court justices. I thought it was interest-

Stewart Glazier is the father of seven children and is currently employed by the Church Educational System as an associate area director, in which capacity he is directly responsible for the supervision of seventy-five seminary teachers. Prior to that he was responsible for the training of new seminary teachers in the Salt Lake Valley as well as writing curriculum materials, and serving as a seminary principal. He recently returned with his family from Santiago, Chile, where he was the mission president. Brother Glazier has been a bishop and a stake president's counselor and is currently serving as a stake president.

ing to see what a judge looked like without his black robe. He looked like any other man, although perhaps a little more dignified.

Judge Struckmeyer explained about suckers, which are shoots that grow as fast as weeds, and about how they needed to be constantly removed in order to allow the vital food resources to go into the tree itself. He explained about weeding and irrigation, which also require constant effort.

Three days later we were called together and told that things were under control, so we wouldn't be needed anymore. "But I would like to keep one of you to look after my orchard," Judge Struckmeyer said, "and maintain it."

Later, when we were alone, Judge Struckmeyer spoke to me: "I needed all six of you in the beginning to help get things into shape. I couldn't tell any of you what I had in mind beforehand, because then you and the others might have put on an act, and I didn't want that. This orchard needs attention, and I don't have the time it takes to keep it in shape. That's where you come in. I've been watching you, as well as the others, and I'm impressed with your concern and dedication. You seem to have a loyalty and intenseness about what you are doing, and I want that. I want someone to look after this orchard as though it were his own. Will you do it?"

What could I say after that? It was a lot of trust for a dollar an hour.

He continued, "I'd like you to submit a weekly timecard with your hours and, in turn, I will mail you your check."

I even got to keep track of my own hours. I couldn't believe it! Just out of high school, and I had that kind of responsibility.

On the way home that night I calculated how much I was going to earn, not only for each day but also for each week, month, and finally for the whole summer. Boy, would Dad be pleased to hear about this!

Four o'clock came early the next morning, but that was part of my proposed schedule. I had estimated that I would need to work ten hours a day, six days a week, in order to meet my goal. For the first week or two things went well and the money accumulated in the bank. Then it seemed as though the sun turned up its volume, and the weeds their growth, and I felt that I needed help.

About this time my cousin Jerry was looking for a job, and he persuaded me to phone Judge Struckmeyer to ask him whether additional help could be hired.

For some reason, I didn't feel good about hiring him. I had had those negative feelings before, but I couldn't think of any logical reason why I shouldn't hire him. My father had taught me to listen to my feelings, but I also knew how Jerry felt, and he needed a job. Finally, I called Judge Struckmeyer.

"Do you feel you really need the help?" Judge Struck-meyer asked.

"Yes, sir. I think so."

"All right, then, but you're responsible."

That thought didn't bother me, and so the two of us worked side by side, battling the weeds and sun.

It was then that I realized that Jerry enjoyed other things more than pulling weeds, one of which was swimming in the canal. And in the heat of the day, I felt it was hard to argue the point. After all, it *was* hot and we didn't seem to waste much time. Besides, as Jerry said, it made us feel like working harder —or so we thought. The cot also became more of a temptation, because we felt that we needed a siesta after our swim.

Three days passed and the weeds began to go unattended. The small tangerine trees saw less and less of us, but the canal enjoyed our company more each day. Several times I half-heartedly tried to persuade Jerry that we should work more and swim less, but I got nowhere with him. In fact, I found myself subscribing more and more to his philosophy as the days turned into weeks.

Then one Friday evening after I returned home from a ward softball game, my mother announced that Judge Struck-meyer had called and wanted to see me at the orchard at eight o'clock sharp the next morning. Fear ran rampant through my body. I didn't have to ask why he wanted to see me; I knew why. Oh, if only I had listened to my father! He had asked me how I felt about hiring Jerry, and I had answered, "Not too good."

"That, my son," he had said, "is the Lord talking, and I suggest you listen."

But Jerry had said he needed the job and I just couldn't let him down. Now I feared the ultimate consequences of that decision; yet still I had the thought that maybe if I got there early the next morning I could get a lot of the work done.

Getting up at three o'clock the next morning was difficult after sleeping in until six or seven every morning. I dressed hurriedly and then started out of the door for Dad's truck.

There were twenty rows of trees in the orchard, each one about 160 feet long, and each was infested with weeds and suckers. I found out fast that repentance is not only slow but also painful and difficult. If I could have been granted a wish that morning, it would have been to skip back in time and to be able to relive the last several weeks, but that couldn't be done.

At about eight o'clock a cloud of dust alerted me to the arrival of Judge Struckmeyer. His car pulled to a stop over by the mesquite trees. As he got out of his car, my eyes could see that he was dressed for farmwork, but in my mind he had on his long, black robe and was ready to step behind the supreme court bench. He walked to the opposite end of the orchard from where I was working and, with his hands behind his back, began to slowly walk up and down the long rows. When he reached the end of one row he turned and began walking up the next. Each row brought him a little bit closer to where I was working. Since four o'clock that morning I had worked on only four rows, and they didn't look good, but they were better than before. Even though the morning was still fairly cool, sweat was running down my face. My heart beat faster and faster as he drew closer and closer.

Finally he turned and started down the row next to mine. By then my heart was ready to jump out of my chest and I wanted to scream, "I'm sorry. It won't happen again."

Slowly he came closer and closer, until he was no more than five feet away from me, just standing there with his hands behind his back. My thoughts traveled back to his words—". . . someone to look after this orchard as though it were his own."

I began working harder and faster, hoping that my industry might bring me a reprieve; but even that was short-lived, for suddenly he broke my turmoil with the words, "I want to see you for a moment."

Dejected and frightened, I followed this great supreme court justice to the "bench" to be sentenced for my negligence. The cot on which we sat was shaded by a twisted mesquite that seemed to be recording everything it saw and heard. Judge Struckmeyer didn't say anything for a moment, and I began to feel that maybe I had impressed him enough to let me have a second chance. I started to open my mouth to apologize when he said, "Stewart, you're fired!" Then he walked to his car, got in, and drove off.

The fruit from that orchard has been picked for years, now. In fact, the grove has been enlarged several times. Judge Struckmeyer has passed away, and even that old mesquite which witnessed the words, "You're fired," has been cut down; but the lesson I learned so profoundly that day still remains: the question is always the same—to whom will you listen? Will it be the still small voice or the persuasions of men?

34

But He That Loseth His Life . . .

NAME WITHHELD

One year into my mission I was assigned, as a district leader, to be the companion of an elder who had been in the mission field four or five months longer than I had. We had both served as senior companions and he seemed somewhat offended that I was to be not only his companion, but also the district leader, which effectively made me his senior companion. It was an awkward situation, and I'm sure it was quite as uncomfortable for him as it was for me. As we began to work together there were a few stumbling blocks, but most of our time together was spent working harmoniously.

One day we were teaching the gospel to a family who had been referred to us by a member of our branch. I had presented the first discussion and had made an appointment to return to teach them the second. After we left their home, my companion said that he just didn't think the family was ready and that we were wasting our time teaching them. I answered that they were the best teaching situation we had at the time and that we had better spend our time working with them.

As we proceeded through the discussions with that family my companion took a passive role in the conversion process. Instead of taking turns teaching the lesson on each visit, he withdrew his participation somewhat, requiring me to give all the discussions and to take the lead in teaching the family. As we continued to teach them they became more and more receptive until, after several weeks, they set a date to be baptized.

The day of the baptism came. That morning, as we were getting ready to leave, I couldn't find the forms we had filled out during the baptismal interviews. I had just seen them a few days before and I knew that we had them, but now they were missing. I asked my companion if he knew where they were and he said that they were in his briefcase. I thought that that was curious, but as we prayed before leaving the apartment it became evident to me that he was planning to take over the final details of the baptism. In other words, after contributing almost nothing to the process, or to the family, he was going to step in and take over some of the most rewarding aspects of the work.

As it dawned on me what was happening I could see the potential for ruining the baptismal day of this family if we were to argue or fight over who was to conduct the interviews and who was to perform the baptisms. I searched my mind and found comfort in the thought that the most important thing was the welfare of the family—that this day should really become a day that they would remember forever. It should be a time for being touched again by the witness of the Spirit, and I knew that that Spirit could not be present when two missionaries were being influenced by the spirit of contention. I did not want to detract from the converts' experience in any way, so I resolved, absolutely, to exert my faith in their behalf so that it would be their special day.

I remember riding along the beach in the open streetcar to the family's home and praying that they would feel the Holy Ghost touch them and testify to them, again, that this was truly the restored gospel. As I did so I felt a sweet confirmation of the Spirit that it would be a wonderful day for them and, in addition, I felt a feeling of personal contentment that I perceived was designed particularly for me. It removed from my soul any bitterness or disappointment at the course my companion had chosen. I did not feel what I had expected to feel. I was at peace. In fact, the influence of the Spirit was so sweet for me that I remember almost arguing with the Lord that what I had been asking was a witness for them, not for me. But he had recognized that two teaching opportunities existed simultaneously—a wonderful family and a young elder. He responded to both.

As we arrived in the family's home I continued that prayer, and when my companion pulled out the paperwork and began the interviews it slowly became evident to them that he would be the one to perform the baptisms that day. I was very supportive of the procedure, and as they looked my way I confirmed that my companion would be doing the baptisms and smiled in the most positive way I knew how. The baptismal interviews proceeded successfully, as did the baptisms. The day turned out to be all that I had prayed for and was, in fact, one that they can look back on as a spiritual milestone.

Now, twenty-seven years later, it is a source of real joy to know that the gospel has become precious to them. Their lives in the intervening years have been exemplary. I thank my Heavenly Father for having had the opportunity of working with this faithful family.

As I reflect back on that day and its events I hold no animosity toward a companion who engaged in some actions that were out of character for him. Instead, I remember that day as one in which we had one of our finest baptisms and in which I felt a deeper understanding of the principle reason why I was a missionary—not to register baptisms in my name, but to lead families to the Savior.